WHAT'S COOKING
chinese

Jenny Stacey

THUNDER BAY
P·R·E·S·S

San Diego, California

Thunder Bay Press
An imprint of the Advantage Publishers Group
5880 Oberlin Drive, San Diego, CA 92121-4794
www.advantagebooksonline.com

Library of Congress Cataloging in Publication Data
Stacey, Jenny.
    What's cooking Chinese / Jenny Stacey.
        p. cm.
    Includes index.
    ISBN 1–57145–153–6
    1. Cookery. Chinese I. Title   98-27333
TX724.5.C5S72 1998   CIP
641.5951--dc21

4 5 6 7 8 06 05 04 03 02

Printed in China

Produced by Haldane Mason, London

Acknowledgments
Art Director: Ron Samuels
Editorial Director: Sydney Francis
Editorial Consultant: Christopher Fagg
Managing Editor: Jo-Anne Cox
Editor: Linda A. Doeser
Design: Digital Artworks Partnership Ltd
Photography: Andrew Sydenham
Home Economist: Kathryn Hawkins
Home Economist's Assistant: Eliza Baird

Note
Unless otherwise stated,
milk is assumed to be full fat, eggs are medium,
and pepper is freshly ground black pepper.

Contents

Introduction

In the West we tend to talk about Chinese cooking as a generalization, as though it were the same throughout China. In fact, China is a vast country, with a range of topography and climates that produce distinct regional differences. The availability of ingredients varies from region to region, and as the Chinese use fresh ingredients in the majority of their cooking, dishes are influenced by availability.

This book contains recipes that are popular in both China and the West. Dishes from Szechuan in the West, Canton in the South, Beijing in the North, and Shanghai in the East offer a wonderful array of different flavors and cooking methods. This book uses the up-to-date cooking methods of China, which produce colorful healthy dishes using simple ingredients and combining color, texture, and flavors well. The dishes included in this book range from hot and spicy to delicate flavors using fish and vegetables, with a mid-range of sweet-and-sour dishes, rice, noodles, and a small section of desserts.

One of the most important features of Chinese cooking is texture. Vegetables should remain crisp, and rice and noodles should be treated like pasta and retain their "bite" after cooking. Ingredients such as bean curd are used for texture, even though they have little flavor in themselves. Bamboo shoots, a common ingredient, are included purely for texture.

Although the Chinese make use of regional, fresh foods, they also use dried foodstuffs in their recipes, in particular mushrooms, bean curd, noodles, and spices. These were first developed to preserve foods, but are now widely used.

REGIONAL VARIATIONS

In Beijing, the cold northerly climate strongly affects the cuisine. There is quite a variety in this region that has inherited influences from the Mandarin courts, and there was also some Manchurian and Mongolian input. Wheat is more popular than rice and many noodle, pancake, and dumpling recipes originate from this area. They also glaze, barbecue, and spit-roast many of their meats. Sauces are robust and rich, using many spices, soy sauce, and garlic. Lamb is the most popular meat in this area as a result of the Mongolian influence.

Cantonese cooking in the South is entirely different. Here, stir-frying produces rich, inventive, and colorful food. Traders and travelers have influenced the cuisine, and the subtropical climate, perfect for fruit-growing, has meant that many savory dishes include fruit, as well as fish and seafood. Very little meat is eaten in the South, although they are famed for their "red" cooking, whereby foods are braised in soy sauce to give a red color. Soy is used extensively here in the thick sauces that are characteristic, and rice is always included in a meal.

In the East, more starch is eaten and considerably more fat is used. Rice is served as an accompaniment or for stuffings. Rice wine is produced and used in abundance, perfectly complementing the range of fish and seafood caught along the coastline. The people of Shanghai have a sweet tooth and savory dishes are much sweeter from this region.

Szechuan cooking from the West is hearty and spicy. They use many chilies and spices, producing hot-and-sour, piquant flavors. Pickles and other preserves feature in the regional cooking, and the foods are traditionally drier, but combine many flavors. Sauces are kept to a minimum, even in stir-fries.

COOKING METHODS

There are several cooking methods used in this book, although very little special equipment is required. The Chinese tend to combine a couple of cooking methods in one dish, such as steaming and then frying, or frying and roasting.

Steaming is widely used in Chinese cooking. Traditionally bamboo steamers are used, so that a whole meal may be cooked in one stack of bamboo racks. The rice is usually placed in the bottom and different dishes stacked on top, those taking the longest to cook being placed at the bottom. If you do not have a steamer, invert a heatproof plate in a large saucepan and cover it with a lid or foil. Boiling water is added to the steamer, to cover one-third of the depth of the dish. This water may need to be replenished during cooking, although many of the dishes cook very quickly. Steaming is a very healthy method of cooking, not using any fat, and it traps the flavors of the dish.

Stir-frying is done in a wok that must be heated before use. Foods of similar size—all small—are stirred constantly, so that as they come into contact with the wok, they cook quickly. Sometimes foods are cooked in batches and removed. This is to preserve flavors. The ingredients are always brought together in the wok at the end of cooking and may have sauces added during or at the end of the cooking time, depending on the region from which they originated. Peanut oil is usually used for stir-frying, but vegetable oil may be used in its place.

Deep-frying is also done in the wok, which uses less oil than a deep-fryer. The shape of the wok allows oil to drain from the food into the center of the wok. The foods are often marinated first or coated in a light batter. **Quick-frying** is also used, whereby foods are either fried on one side (used for noodles) and not turned, or turned once and sliced for serving.

INGREDIENTS

Most of the recipes in this book use ingredients readily available in western supermarkets, but more traditional options have been suggested where appropriate. It is worth making a trip to a Chinese grocery store for high-quality soy sauce and some of the other slightly more obscure ingredients, but the recipes will all work very well and be equally delicious without them.

Bamboo shoots *These are added purely for texture, as they have very little flavor. Available in cans, they are a common ingredient in Chinese cooking.*

Bean curd *This soy bean paste is available in several forms. The cake variety, which is soft and spongy and a white-gray color, is used in this book. It is very bland, but adds texture to dishes and is perfect for absorbing all the other flavors in the dish.*

Bean sprouts *These are mung bean shoots, which are very nutritious, containing many vitamins. They add crunch to a recipe and are widely available. Do not overcook them, as they wilt and do not add texture to the dish.*

Black beans *These are soy beans and are very salty. They can be bought and crushed with salt and then rinsed or used in the form of a ready-made sauce for convenience.*

Chinese beans *These long beans may be eaten whole and are very tender. Green beans may also be used.*

Chinese five-spice powder *An aromatic blend of cinnamon, cloves, star anise, fennel, and brown peppercorns. It is often used in marinades.*

Chinese cabbage *A light green leaf with a sweet flavor. It can be found in most supermarkets.*

Cilantro *Also known as Chinese parsley, this has a strong, pungent flavor. Use it sparingly to avoid overpowering the other ingredients in a dish.*

Hoisin sauce *A dark brown, sweet, thick sauce that is widely available. It is made from spices, soy sauce, garlic, and chili and is often served as a dipping sauce.*

Litchis *These are worth buying fresh, as they are easy to prepare. Inside the inedible skin is a fragrant white fruit. Litchis are available canned and are a classic ingredient.*

Mango *Choose a ripe mango and delight in the sweet, scented flesh. If a mango is underripe when bought, leave it in a sunny place for a few days before using.*

Noodles *The Chinese use several varieties of noodle. You will probably find it easier to use the readily available dried varieties, such as egg noodles, which are yellow, rice stick noodles, which are white and very fine, or cellophane noodles, which are opaque when dry and turn transparent on cooking. These may not be easy to find, and rice noodles may be used instead.*

Oyster sauce *Readily available, this sauce is made from oysters, salt, seasonings, and cornstarch, and is brown in color.*

Bok choy *Also known as Chinese cabbage, this has a mild, slightly bitter flavor. It is available from supermarkets.*

Rice vinegar *This has a mild, sweet taste that is quite delicate. It is available in some supermarkets and is well worth obtaining. If it is not available, use cider vinegar.*

Rice wine *This is similar to dry sherry in color, alcohol content, and smell, but it is worth buying rice wine for its distinctive flavor.*

Sesame oil *This is made from roasted sesame seeds and has an intense flavor. It burns easily and is therefore added right at the end of cooking for flavor, and is not used for frying.*

Soy sauce *This is widely available, but it is worth buying a good grade of sauce. It is produced in both light and dark varieties—the former is used with fish and vegetables for a lighter color and flavor, while the latter, being darker, richer, saltier, and more intense, is used as a dipping sauce or with strongly flavored meats.*

Star anise *This is an eight-pointed, star-shaped pod with a strong aniseed flavor. The spice is also available ground. If a pod is added to a dish during cooking, it should be removed before serving.*

Szechuan pepper *This is quite hot and spicy and should be used sparingly. It is red in color and is readily available from Chinese grocery stores.*

Water chestnuts *These are flat and round and can usually only be purchased in cans, already peeled. They add a delicious crunch to dishes and have a sweet flavor.*

Yellow beans *Again a soy bean and very salty. Yellow bean sauce has been used in this book, and it is suggested you purchase a good variety that is chunky rather than smooth.*

Soups & Starters

In China soups are not usually served at the beginning of a meal but between courses to clear the palate. It is also quite common for Chinese families to serve a large tureen of clear soup at the same time as the other dishes. The soups in this chapter bring a whole range of flavors and textures to the table. There are thicker soups, thin clear consommés, and those topped with wontons for effect and flavor. These soups can be eaten as a lunch or snack on their own—whatever your preference, they all taste delicious!

The starters in this chapter are a combination of old favorites and traditional Chinese dishes, and there is sure to be something to suit every occasion. One of the advantages of these dishes is that they can be prepared and cooked in advance. Instead of serving the starters individually, try serving a small portion of each together as an assorted hors d'oeuvre. Remember not to have more than one of the same type of food—the ingredients should be chosen for their harmony and balance in color, aroma, flavor, and texture.

Clear Chicken & Egg Soup

This tasty chicken soup has the addition of poached eggs, making it both delicious and filling. Use fresh, homemade chicken stock for a better flavor.

Serves 4

INGREDIENTS

1 tsp salt
1 tbsp rice wine vinegar
4 eggs
3³/₄ cups chicken stock
1 leek, sliced

4¹/₂ ounces broccoli florets
1 cup shredded
   cooked chicken
2 open-cap mushrooms, sliced
1 tbsp dry sherry

dash of chili sauce
chili powder, to garnish

1 Bring a large saucepan of water to a boil and add the salt and rice wine vinegar. Reduce the heat so that it is just simmering and carefully break the eggs into the water, one at a time. Poach the eggs for 1 minute. Remove the poached eggs with a slotted spoon and set aside.

2 Bring the chicken stock to a boil in a separate pan and add the leek, broccoli, chicken, mushrooms, and sherry, and season with chili sauce to taste. Cook for 10–15 minutes.

3 Add the poached eggs to the soup and cook for a further 2 minutes. Carefully transfer the soup and poached eggs to 4 individual soup bowls. Dust with a little chili powder to garnish and serve immediately.

VARIATION

You could substitute 4½ ounces fresh or canned crab meat or the same quantity of fresh or frozen cooked shrimp for the chicken, if desired.

VARIATION

You could use 4 dried Chinese mushrooms, rehydrated according to the package instructions, instead of the open-cap mushrooms, if desired.

Curried Chicken & Corn Soup

Tender cooked chicken strips and baby corncobs are the main flavors in this delicious clear soup, with just a hint of ginger.

Serves 4

INGREDIENTS

6 ounce can corn, drained

3³/₄ cups chicken stock

12 ounces cooked, lean chicken, cut into strips

16 baby corncobs

1 tsp Chinese curry powder

¹/₂-inch piece fresh ginger root, grated

3 tbsp light soy sauce

2 tbsp chopped chives

1 Place the canned corn in a food processor, together with ²/₃ cup of the chicken stock and process until the mixture forms a smooth purée.

2 Rub the corn purée through a fine strainer, pressing with the back of a spoon to remove any husks.

3 Pour the remaining chicken stock into a large saucepan and add the strips of cooked chicken. Stir in the corn purée.

4 Add the baby corncobs and bring the soup to a boil. Boil the soup for 10 minutes.

5 Add the curry powder, grated ginger, and soy sauce and cook for a further 10–15 minutes. Stir in the chopped chives.

6 Transfer the soup to warm individual soup bowls and serve immediately.

COOK'S TIP

Prepare the soup up to 24 hours in advance without adding the chicken, cool, cover, and store in the refrigerator. Add the chicken and heat the soup through thoroughly before serving.

Hot & Sour Soup

This well-known soup from Beijing is easy to make and very filling. It is often eaten as a meal on its own and should be served before a light menu if it is offered as an appetizer.

Serves 4

INGREDIENTS

2 tbsp cornstarch
4 tbsp water
2 tbsp light soy sauce
3 tbsp rice wine vinegar
1/2 tsp ground black pepper

1 small fresh red chili,
    finely chopped
1 egg
2 tbsp vegetable oil
1 onion, chopped

3 3/4 cups chicken or beef consommé
1 open-cap mushroom, sliced
1 3/4 ounces skinless chicken breast,
    cut into very thin strips
1 tsp sesame oil

1 Blend the cornstarch with the water to form a smooth paste. Add the soy sauce, rice wine vinegar, pepper, and chili and mix together well.

2 Break the egg into a separate bowl and beat well.

3 Heat the oil in a preheated wok and stir-fry the onion for 1–2 minutes.

4 Stir in the consommé, mushroom, and chicken and bring to a boil. Cook for about 15 minutes, or until the chicken is tender.

5 Pour the cornstarch mixture into the soup and cook the soup, stirring constantly, until it has thickened.

6 As you are stirring, gradually drizzle the egg into the soup, to create threads of egg.

7 Sprinkle with the sesame oil and serve immediately.

COOK'S TIP

Make sure that the egg is poured in very slowly and that you stir continuously to create threads of egg and not large pieces.

Peking Duck Soup

This is a hearty and robustly flavored soup, containing pieces of duck and vegetables cooked in a rich stock.

Serves 4

INGREDIENTS

4¹/₂ ounces lean duck breast
8 ounces Chinese cabbage
3³/₄ cups chicken or duck stock
1 tbsp dry sherry or rice wine

1 tbsp light soy sauce
2 garlic cloves, crushed
pinch of ground star anise
1 tbsp sesame seeds

1 tsp sesame oil
1 tbsp chopped fresh parsley

1 Remove the skin from the duck breast and finely dice the flesh.

2 Using a sharp knife, shred the Chinese cabbage.

3 Put the stock in a large saucepan and bring to a boil.

4 Add the sherry or rice wine, soy sauce, diced duck meat, and shredded Chinese cabbage and stir to mix thoroughly. Reduce the heat and simmer gently for 15 minutes.

5 Stir in the garlic and star anise and cook over a low heat for a further 10–15 minutes, or until the duck is tender.

6 Meanwhile, dry-fry the sesame seeds in a preheated, heavy-based skillet or wok, stirring constantly.

7 Remove the sesame seeds from the pan and stir them into the soup, together with the sesame oil and parsley.

8 Spoon the soup into warm bowls and serve immediately.

COOK'S TIP

If Chinese cabbage is unavailable, use leafy green cabbage instead. You may wish to adjust the quantity to taste, as Western cabbage has a stronger flavor and odor than Chinese cabbage.

Beef & Vegetable Noodle Soup

Thin strips of beef are marinated in soy sauce and garlic to form the basis of this delicious soup. Served with noodles, it is both filling and delicious.

Serves 4

INGREDIENTS

8 ounces lean beef
1 garlic clove, crushed
2 scallions, chopped
3 tbsp soy sauce
1 tsp sesame oil

8 ounces egg noodles
$3^3/4$ cups beef stock
3 baby corncobs, sliced
$^1/2$ leek, shredded

$4^1/2$ ounces broccoli, cut
 into florets
pinch of chili powder

1 Using a sharp knife, cut the beef into very thin strips and place them in a shallow glass bowl or dish.

2 Add the garlic, scallions, soy sauce, and sesame oil and mix together well, turning the beef to coat. Cover and marinate in the refrigerator for 30 minutes.

3 Cook the noodles in a saucepan of boiling water for 3–4 minutes. Drain the noodles thoroughly and set aside until they are required.

4 Put the beef stock in a large saucepan and bring to a boil.

5 Add the beef, together with the marinade, the baby corn, leek, and broccoli. Cover and simmer over a low heat for 7–10 minutes, or until the beef and vegetables are tender and cooked through.

6 Stir in the noodles and chili powder and cook for a further 2–3 minutes. Transfer to bowls and serve immediately.

COOK'S TIP

Vary the vegetables used, or use those on hand. If desired, use a few drops of chili sauce instead of chili powder, but remember it is very hot!

Lamb & Rice Soup

This is a very filling soup, as it contains rice and tender pieces of lamb.
Serve before a light main course.

Serves 4

INGREDIENTS

5¹/₂ ounces lean lamb
¹/₄ cup rice
3³/₄ cups lamb stock
1 leek, sliced

1 garlic clove, thinly sliced
2 tsp light soy sauce
1 tsp rice wine vinegar

1 medium open-cap mushroom,
   thinly sliced
salt

1 Using a sharp knife, trim any fat from the lamb and cut the meat into thin strips. Set aside until required.

2 Bring a large pan of lightly salted water to a boil and add the rice. Bring back to a boil, stir once, reduce the heat, and cook for 10–15 minutes, until tender. Drain, rinse under cold running water, drain again, and set aside until required.

3 Meanwhile, put the lamb stock in a large saucepan and bring to a boil.

4 Add the lamb strips, leek, garlic, soy sauce, and rice wine vinegar to the stock in the pan. Reduce the heat, cover, and simmer for 10 minutes, or until the lamb is tender and thoroughly cooked through.

5 Add the mushroom slices and the rice to the pan and cook for a further 2–3 minutes, or until the mushroom is completely cooked through.

6 Ladle the soup into 4 individual warm soup bowls and serve immediately.

VARIATION

Use a few dried Chinese mushrooms, rehydrated according to the package instructions and chopped, as an alternative to the open-cap mushroom. Add the Chinese mushrooms with the lamb in step 4.

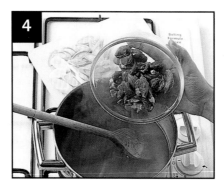

Fish Soup with Wontons

This soup is topped with small wontons filled with shrimp,
making it both very tasty and satisfying.

Serves 4

INGREDIENTS

4¹/₂ ounces large, cooked, peeled
   shrimp
1 tsp chopped chives
1 small garlic clove, finely chopped

1 tbsp vegetable oil
12 wonton wrappers
1 small egg, beaten
3³/₄ cups fish stock

6 ounces white fish fillet, diced
dash of chili sauce
sliced fresh red chili and chives,
   to garnish

1 Roughly chop about one quarter of the shrimp and mix together with the chopped chives and garlic.

2 Heat the oil in a preheated wok and stir-fry the shrimp mixture for 1–2 minutes. Remove from the heat and set aside to cool completely.

3 Spread out the wonton wrappers on a counter. Spoon a little of the shrimp filling into the center of each wrapper. Brush the edges of the wrappers with beaten egg and press the edges

together, scrunching them to form a "moneybag" shape. Set the wontons aside while you are preparing the soup.

4 Pour the fish stock into a large saucepan and bring to a boil. Add the diced white fish and the remaining shrimp and cook for 5 minutes.

5 Season to taste with the chili sauce. Add the wontons and cook for a further 5 minutes. Spoon into warm serving bowls, garnish with sliced red chili and chives, and serve immediately.

VARIATION

Replace the shrimp with cooked crab meat for an alternative flavor.

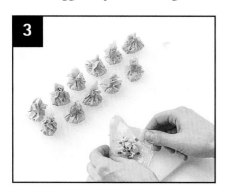

Crab & Ginger Soup

*Two classic ingredients in Chinese cooking are blended together
in this recipe for a special soup.*

Serves 4

INGREDIENTS

1 carrot, peeled and chopped
1 leek, chopped
1 bay leaf
3³/4 cups fish stock

2 medium-size cooked crabs
1-inch piece fresh ginger root, grated
1 tsp light soy sauce

¹/2 tsp ground star anise
salt and pepper

1 Put the carrot, leek, bay leaf, and fish stock into a large saucepan and bring to a boil. Reduce the heat, cover, and simmer for about 10 minutes, or until the carrot and leek are nearly tender.

2 Meanwhile, remove all of the meat from the cooked crabs. Break off the claws and legs, break the joints, and remove the meat (you may require a fork for this). Discard the gills, split the bodies open, and scoop out all the meat. Add the crab meat to the saucepan of fish stock.

3 Add the ginger, soy sauce, and star anise to the fish stock and bring to a boil. Simmer for about 10 minutes, or until the vegetables are tender and the crab is heated through. Season to taste with salt and pepper. Ladle the soup into warm individual bowls and serve immediately.

COOK'S TIP

If fresh crab meat is unavailable, use drained canned crab meat or thawed frozen crab meat instead.

COOK'S TIP

To prepare cooked crab, loosen the meat from the shell by banging the back of the underside with a clenched fist. Stand the crab on its edge with the shell toward you. Force the shell from the body with your thumbs. Twist off the legs and claws and remove the meat. Twist off the tail and discard. Remove and discard the gills from each side of the body. Cut the body in half along the center and remove all of the meat. Scoop the brown meat from the shell with a spoon.

Shrimp Dumpling Soup

These small dumplings filled with shrimp and pork may be made slightly larger and served as dim sum *on their own, if desired.*

Serves 4

INGREDIENTS

DUMPLINGS:
1 5/8 cups all-purpose flour
1/4 cup boiling water
1/8 cup cold water
1 1/2 tsp vegetable oil

FILLING:
4 1/2 ounces ground pork
4 1/2 ounces cooked, peeled
  shrimp, chopped
1 3/4 ounces canned water chestnuts,
  drained, rinsed, and chopped
1 celery stalk, chopped
1 tsp cornstarch

1 tbsp sesame oil
1 tbsp light soy sauce

SOUP:
3 3/4 cups fish stock
1 3/4 ounces cellophane noodles
1 tbsp dry sherry
chopped chives, to garnish

1 To make the dumplings, mix together the flour, boiling water, cold water, and oil in a bowl until a pliable dough is formed.

2 Knead the dough on a lightly floured surface for 5 minutes. Cut the dough into 16 equal-size pieces.

3 Roll the dough pieces into rounds about 3 inches in diameter.

4 Mix the filling ingredients together in a large bowl.

5 Spoon a little of the filling mixture into the center of each round. Bring the edges of the dough together, scrunching them up to form a "moneybag" shape. Twist to seal.

6 Pour the fish stock into a large saucepan and bring to a boil.

7 Add the cellophane noodles, dumplings, and dry sherry to the pan and cook for 4–5 minutes, until the noodles and dumplings are tender. Garnish with chopped chives and serve immediately.

COOK'S TIP

Wonton wrappers may be used instead of the dumpling dough if time is short.

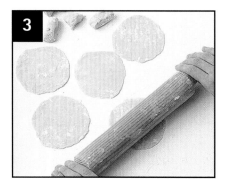

Chinese Cabbage Soup

This is a piquant soup, which is slightly sweet-and-sour in flavor. Chinese cabbage is cooked in a vegetable broth with sugar, vinegar, and chili and served as a hearty meal or appetizer.

Serves 4

INGREDIENTS

1 pound bok choy
2 1/2 cups vegetable stock
1 tbsp rice wine vinegar
1 tbsp light soy sauce

1 tbsp superfine sugar
1 tbsp dry sherry
1 fresh red chili, thinly sliced

1 tbsp cornstarch
2 tbsp water

1 Using a sharp knife, trim the stems of the bok choy and shred the leaves.

2 Heat the stock in a large saucepan. Add the bok choy and cook for 10–15 minutes.

3 Mix the rice wine vinegar, soy sauce, sugar, and sherry together. Add this mixture to the stock, together with the sliced chili. Bring to a boil, lower the heat, and cook for 2–3 minutes.

4 Blend the cornstarch with the water to form a smooth paste.

Gradually stir the cornstarch mixture into the soup. Cook, stirring constantly, until it has thickened. Cook for a further 4–5 minutes. Ladle the soup into individual warm serving bowls and serve immediately.

VARIATION

Boil about 2 tbsp rice in lightly salted water until tender. Drain and spoon into the base of the soup bowls. Ladle the soup over the rice and serve immediately.

COOK'S TIP

Bok choy, *also known as* pak choi *or spoon cabbage, has long, white leaf stalks and fleshy, spoon-shaped, shiny green leaves. There are a number of varieties available, which differ mainly in size rather than flavor.*

Spring Rolls

This classic Chinese dish is very popular in the West.
Serve hot or chilled with a soy sauce or hoisin dip.

Serves 4

INGREDIENTS

6 ounces cooked pork, chopped
$2^3/4$ ounces cooked chicken, chopped
1 tsp light soy sauce
1 tsp light brown sugar
1 tsp sesame oil
1 tsp vegetable oil
8 ounces bean sprouts

1 ounce canned bamboo shoots,
   drained, rinsed, and chopped
1 green bell pepper, seeded and chopped
2 scallions, sliced
1 tsp cornstarch
2 tsp water
vegetable oil, for deep-frying

SKINS:
$1^1/8$ cups all-purpose flour
5 tbsp cornstarch
2 cups water
3 tbsp vegetable oil

1 Mix the pork, chicken, soy sauce, sugar, and sesame oil. Cover and marinate for 30 minutes.

2 Heat the oil in a preheated wok. Stir-fry the bean sprouts, bamboo shoots, bell pepper, and scallions for 2–3 minutes. Add the meat and the marinade and stir-fry for a further 2–3 minutes.

3 Blend the cornstarch with the water and stir the mixture

into the wok. Set aside to cool completely.

4 To make the skins, mix the flour and cornstarch, and gradually stir in the water to make a smooth batter.

5 Heat a small, oiled skillet. Swirl one-eighth of the batter over the base and cook for 2–3 minutes. Repeat with the remaining batter. Cover with a damp dish cloth.

6 Spread out the skins and spoon one-eighth of the filling along the center of each. Brush the edges with water and fold in the sides, then roll up.

7 Heat the oil for deep-frying in a wok until a cube of bread browns in 30 seconds. Cook the spring rolls, in batches, for 2–3 minutes, or until golden and crisp. Remove from the oil and drain on absorbent paper towels. Transfer to a serving dish and serve at once.

Pork Dim Sum

*These small steamed packets are traditionally served as an appetizer
and are very adaptable to your favorite fillings.*

Serves 4

INGREDIENTS

14 ounces ground pork
2 scallions, chopped
1³/4 ounces canned bamboo shoots,
   drained, rinsed, and chopped

1 tbsp light soy sauce
1 tbsp dry sherry
2 tsp sesame oil
2 tsp superfine sugar

1 egg white, lightly beaten
4¹/2 tsp cornstarch
24 wonton wrappers

1 Mix together the ground pork, chopped scallions, bamboo shoots, soy sauce, dry sherry, sesame oil, sugar, and beaten egg white in a bowl until well combined.

2 Stir in the cornstarch, mixing thoroughly.

3 Spread out the wonton wrappers on a counter. Place a spoonful of the pork and vegetable mixture in the center of each wonton wrapper and lightly brush the edges of the wrappers with water.

4 Bring the sides of the wrappers together in the center of the filling, pinching firmly together.

5 Line a steamer with a clean, damp dish cloth and arrange the wontons inside. Cover and steam for 5–7 minutes, until cooked through. Serve.

COOK'S TIP

Bamboo steamers are designed to rest on the sloping sides of a wok above the water. They are available in a range of sizes.

VARIATION

Use shrimp, ground chicken, or crab meat for the filling, with other vegetables, such as chopped carrot, and flavorings, such as chili or ginger, if desired.

Crispy Crab Wontons

These delicious wontons are a superb appetizer. Deep-fried until crisp and golden, they are delicious with a chili dipping sauce.

Serves 4

INGREDIENTS

6 ounces white crab meat, flaked
1³/4 ounces canned water chestnuts,
  drained, rinsed, and chopped
1 small fresh red chili, chopped

1 scallion, chopped
1 tbsp cornstarch
1 tsp dry sherry
1 tsp light soy sauce

¹/2 tsp lime juice
24 wonton wrappers
vegetable oil, for deep-frying
sliced lime, to garnish

1 To make the filling, mix together the crab meat, water chestnuts, chili, scallion, cornstarch, sherry, soy sauce, and lime juice in a bowl.

2 Spread out the wonton wrappers on a counter and spoon one portion of the crab meat filling into the center of each wonton wrapper.

3 Dampen the edges of the wonton wrappers with a little water and fold them in half to form triangles. Fold the two pointed ends in toward the center, moisten with a little water to secure, and then pinch together to seal.

4 Heat the oil for deep-frying in a wok or deep-fryer until a cube of bread browns in 30 seconds. Fry the wontons, in batches, for 2–3 minutes, until golden brown and crisp. Remove the wontons from the oil with a slotted spoon and drain on paper towels.

5 Transfer the wontons to a serving dish, garnish with slices of lime, and serve hot.

COOK'S TIP

Wonton wrappers, available from Chinese grocery stores, are paper-thin squares made from wheat flour and egg. They can be easily damaged, so handle them carefully. Make sure that the wontons are sealed well before deep-frying to prevent the filling from coming out and the wontons unwrapping.

Pot Sticker Dumplings

These dumplings obtain their name from the fact that they would stick to the pot when steamed if they were not fried crisply enough initially.

Serves 4

INGREDIENTS

DUMPLINGS:
1$\frac{1}{2}$ cups all-purpose flour
pinch of salt
3 tbsp vegetable oil
6–8 tbsp boiling water
oil, for deep-frying
sliced scallions and chives, to garnish

FILLING:
5$\frac{1}{2}$ ounces lean chicken, very finely chopped
1 ounce canned bamboo shoots, drained and chopped
2 scallions, finely chopped
$\frac{1}{2}$ small red bell pepper, seeded and finely chopped
$\frac{1}{2}$ tsp Chinese curry powder

1 tbsp light soy sauce
1 tsp superfine sugar
1 tsp sesame oil

1 To make the dumplings, mix together the flour and salt in a bowl. Make a well in the center, add the oil and water, and mix well to form a soft dough. Knead the dough on a lightly floured surface, wrap in plastic wrap, and let stand for 30 minutes.

2 Meanwhile, put all the filling ingredients in a large bowl and mix thoroughly.

3 Divide the dough into 12 equal-size pieces and roll each piece into a 5-inch round. Spoon a portion of the filling onto one half of each round.

4 Fold the dough over the filling to form a "turnover," pressing the edges together to seal.

5 Pour a little oil into a heavy-based skillet and cook the dumplings, in batches, until browned and slightly crisp.

6 Drain the oil from the skillet. Return all of the dumplings to the skillet and add about $\frac{1}{2}$ cup water. Cover and steam for 5 minutes, or until the dumplings are cooked through. Remove with a slotted spoon and transfer to a serving dish. Garnish and serve with soy or hoisin sauce.

Pancake Rolls

This is another classic dim sum *dish that is adaptable to almost any filling of your choice. Here the traditional mixture of pork and bok choy is used.*

Serves 4

INGREDIENTS

4 tsp vegetable oil
1–2 garlic cloves, crushed
8 ounces ground pork
8 ounces bok choy, shredded

4¹/₂ tsp light soy sauce
¹/₂ tsp sesame oil
8 spring roll skins, 10 inches square,
   thawed if frozen

oil, for deep-frying
chili sauce (see Cook's Tip, below),
   to serve

1 Heat the vegetable oil in a preheated wok. Add the garlic and stir-fry for 30 seconds. Add the pork and stir-fry for about 2–3 minutes, until just becoming lightly colored.

2 Add the shredded bok choy, soy sauce, and sesame oil to the wok and stir-fry for 2–3 minutes. Remove from the heat and set aside to cool.

3 Spread out the spring roll skins on a counter and spoon 2 tablespoons of the pork mixture along one edge of each. Roll the skin over once and fold in the sides. Roll up completely to make a sausage shape, brushing the edges with a little water to seal. If you have time, set the pancake rolls aside for 10 minutes to seal firmly.

4 Heat the oil for deep-frying in a wok until almost smoking. Reduce the heat slightly and fry the pancake rolls, in batches if necessary, for 3–4 minutes, until golden brown. Remove from the oil with a slotted spoon and drain on paper towels. Serve at once with chili sauce.

COOK'S TIP

To make chili sauce, heat ¼ cup superfine sugar, ¼ cup rice vinegar, and 2 tablespoons water in a small saucepan, stirring until the sugar has dissolved. Bring the mixture to a boil and boil rapidly until a light syrup forms. Remove the pan from the heat and stir in 2 finely chopped, fresh red chilies. Let the sauce cool before serving. If you prefer a milder dipping sauce, seed the chilies before chopping them.

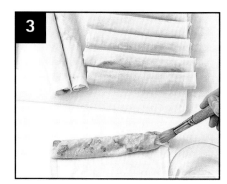

Sesame Shrimp Toasts

These small toasts are easy to prepare and are one of the most popular Chinese appetizers in the West. Make sure you serve plenty of them as they are very tasty!

Serves 4

INGREDIENTS

8 ounces cooked, peeled shrimp
1 scallion
1/4 tsp salt
1 tsp light soy sauce

1 tbsp cornstarch
1 egg white, beaten

3 thin slices white bread,
    crusts removed
4 tbsp sesame seeds
vegetable oil, for deep-frying

1 Put the shrimp and scallion in a food processor and process until finely ground. Alternatively, chop them very finely. Transfer to a bowl and stir in the salt, soy sauce, cornstarch, and egg white.

2 Spread the mixture onto one side of each slice of bread. Spread the sesame seeds on top of the mixture, pressing down well.

3 Cut each slice of coated bread into four equal triangles or into strips.

4 Heat the oil for deep-frying in a wok until almost smoking. Carefully place the triangles in the oil, coated side down, and cook for 2–3 minutes, until golden brown. Remove with a slotted spoon and drain on paper towels. Transfer to a serving dish and serve hot.

VARIATION

If desired, you could add ½ tsp very finely chopped fresh ginger root and 1 tsp Chinese rice wine to the shrimp mixture at the end of step 1.

COOK'S TIP

Fry the triangles in two batches, keeping the first batch warm while you cook the second, to prevent them from sticking together and overcooking.

Sweet & Sour Fried Shrimp

These delicious shrimp are marinated in a soy sauce mixture before being coated in a light batter, fried, and served with a delicious sweet-and-sour dip.

Serves 4

INGREDIENTS

16 large raw shrimp, peeled
1 tsp grated fresh ginger root
1 garlic clove, crushed
2 scallions, sliced
2 tbsp dry sherry
2 tsp sesame oil
1 tbsp light soy sauce
vegetable oil, for deep-frying
shredded scallion,
   to garnish

BATTER:
4 egg whites
4 tbsp cornstarch
2 tbsp all-purpose flour

SAUCE:
2 tbsp tomato paste
3 tbsp white wine vinegar
4 tsp light soy sauce
2 tbsp lemon juice

3 tbsp light brown sugar
1 green bell pepper, seeded and cut
   into thin matchsticks
$^1/_2$ tsp chili sauce
$1^1/_4$ cups vegetable stock
2 tsp cornstarch

1 Using tweezers, devein the shrimp, then flatten them with a large knife.

2 Place the shrimp in a shallow dish and add the ginger, garlic, scallions, sherry, sesame oil, and soy sauce. Cover and marinate 30 minutes.

3 Make the batter by beating the egg whites until thick. Fold in the cornstarch and flour to form a light batter.

4 Place all the sauce ingredients in a pan and bring to a boil. Reduce the heat and simmer for 10 minutes.

5 Remove the shrimp from the marinade and dip them into the batter to coat.

6 Heat the oil until almost smoking. Reduce the heat and fry the shrimp for about 3–4 minutes, until crisp and golden brown. Serve with the sauce.

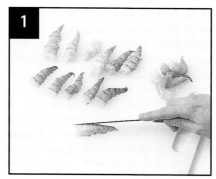

Shrimp Rice Paper Packets

Special rice paper wrappers are available in Chinese grocery stores and health food stores. Do not use the rice paper sold for making cakes.

Serves 4

INGREDIENTS

1 egg white
2 tsp cornstarch
2 tsp dry sherry
1 tsp superfine sugar
2 tsp hoisin sauce

8 ounces peeled, cooked shrimp
4 scallions, sliced
1 ounce canned water chestnuts, drained, rinsed, and chopped
8 Chinese rice paper wrappers

vegetable oil, for deep-frying
hoisin sauce or plum sauce, to serve

1 Lightly beat the egg white, then mix in the cornstarch, dry sherry, superfine sugar, and hoisin sauce. Add the shrimp, sliced scallions, and water chestnuts, mixing together thoroughly.

2 Soften the rice papers by dipping them in a bowl of water one at a time. Spread them out on a counter.

3 Spoon a little of the shrimp mixture into the center of each rice paper and wrap the paper around the filling to make a secure packet.

4 Heat the oil in a wok until it is almost smoking. Reduce the heat slightly, add the packets, in batches if necessary, and deep-fry for 4–5 minutes, until crisp. Remove from the oil with a slotted spoon and drain on absorbent paper towels.

5 Transfer the packets to a warm serving dish and serve immediately with a little hoisin or plum sauce.

COOK'S TIP

Use this filling inside wonton wrappers (see page 30) if the rice paper wrappers are unavailable.

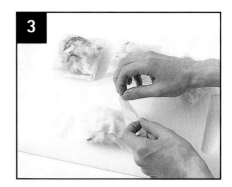

Crab Ravioli

These small packets are made with wonton wrappers, filled with mixed vegetables and crab meat, and cooked to perfection for a melt-in-your-mouth appetizer.

Serves 4

INGREDIENTS

1 pound crab meat (fresh or canned and drained)

$1/2$ red bell pepper, seeded and finely diced

$4^1/2$ ounces Chinese cabbage, shredded

1 ounce bean sprouts, roughly chopped

1 tbsp light soy sauce

1 tsp lime juice

16 wonton wrappers

1 small egg, beaten

2 tbsp peanut oil

1 tsp sesame oil

salt and pepper

1 Mix together the crab meat, bell pepper, Chinese cabbage, bean sprouts, soy sauce, and lime juice in a bowl. Season and let stand for 15 minutes, stirring the mixture occasionally.

2 Spread out the wonton wrappers on a counter. Spoon a little of the crab meat mixture into the center of each wrapper, dividing it equally among them.

3 Brush the edges of the wrappers with the beaten egg and fold in half, pushing out any air. Press the edges together with your fingers to seal tightly.

4 Heat the peanut oil in a preheated wok or heavy-based skillet. Fry the ravioli, in batches, for 3–4 minutes, turning until browned. Remove with a slotted spoon and drain thoroughly on paper towels.

5 Heat the remaining filling in the wok or skillet over a gentle heat until hot. Serve the ravioli with the hot filling and sprinkled with sesame oil.

COOK'S TIP

Make sure that the edges of the ravioli are sealed well and that all of the air is pressed out to prevent them from opening during cooking.

Spareribs

Another classic favorite in Chinese restaurants, these sticky ribs are best eaten with your fingers.

Serves 4

INGREDIENTS

2 pounds pork spareribs
2 tbsp dark soy sauce
3 tbsp hoisin sauce

1 tbsp Chinese rice wine or dry sherry
pinch of Chinese five-spice powder
2 tsp dark brown sugar

1/4 tsp chili sauce
2 garlic cloves, crushed
cilantro sprigs, to garnish (optional)

1 Cut the spareribs into separate pieces if they are joined together. If desired, you can chop them into 2-inch lengths.

2 Mix together the soy sauce, hoisin sauce, Chinese rice wine or sherry, Chinese five-spice powder, dark brown sugar, chili sauce, and garlic in a large bowl.

3 Place the ribs in a shallow dish and pour the mixture over them, turning to make sure they are well coated. Cover and marinate in the refrigerator, turning the ribs from time to time, for at least 1 hour.

4 Remove the ribs from the marinade and arrange them in a single layer on a wire rack placed over a roasting pan half filled with warm water. Brush with the marinade, reserving the remainder.

5 Cook in a preheated oven at 350°F for 30 minutes. Remove the roasting pan from the oven and turn the ribs over. Brush with the remaining marinade and return to the oven for a further 30 minutes, or until cooked through. Transfer to a warm serving dish, garnish with the cilantro sprigs (if using), and serve the ribs immediately.

COOK'S TIP

Add more hot water to the roasting pan during cooking if required. Do not allow it to dry out, as the water steams the ribs and aids in their cooking.

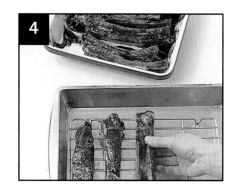

Honeyed Chicken Wings

Chicken wings are ideal as an appetizer, as they are small and perfect for eating with the fingers.

Serves 4

INGREDIENTS

1 pound chicken wings
2 tbsp peanut oil
2 tbsp light soy sauce
2 tbsp hoisin sauce
2 tbsp clear honey

2 garlic cloves, crushed
1 tsp sesame seeds

MARINADE:
1 dried red chili
$1/2$–1 tsp chili powder
$1/2$–1 tsp ground ginger
finely grated rind of 1 lime

1 To make the marinade, crush the dried chili in a mortar with a pestle. Mix together the crushed dried chili, chili powder, ground ginger, and lime rind in a small mixing bowl.

2 Thoroughly rub the spice mixture into the chicken wings with your fingertips. Set aside for at least 2 hours to allow the flavors to penetrate the chicken wings.

3 Heat the peanut oil in a preheated wok.

4 Add the chicken wings and fry, turning frequently, for 10–12 minutes, until golden and crisp. Drain off any excess oil.

5 Add the soy sauce, hoisin sauce, honey, garlic, and sesame seeds to the wok, turning the chickens wings to coat them with the mixture.

6 Reduce the heat and cook for 20–25 minutes, turning the chicken wings frequently, until completely cooked through. Serve hot.

COOK'S TIP

Make the dish in advance and freeze the chicken wings. Thaw thoroughly, cover with foil, and heat through in a moderate oven.

Steamed Duck Buns

*The dough used in this recipe may be wrapped around a wide variety of fillings,
such as chicken, pork, or shrimp, or sweet fillings as an alternative.*

Serves 4

INGREDIENTS

DUMPLING DOUGH:
$2^2/_3$ cups all-purpose flour
$^1/_2$ ounce dried yeast
1 tsp superfine sugar
2 tbsp warm water
$^3/_4$ cup warm milk

FILLING:
$10^1/_2$ ounces duck breast
1 tbsp light brown sugar
1 tbsp light soy sauce
2 tbsp clear honey
1 tbsp hoisin sauce
1 tbsp vegetable oil

1 leek, finely chopped
1 garlic clove, crushed
$^1/_2$-inch piece fresh ginger
root, grated

1 Place the duck breast in a large bowl. Mix together the sugar, soy sauce, honey, and hoisin sauce. Pour the mixture over the duck and marinate for 20 minutes.

2 Remove the duck from the marinade and cook on a rack set over a roasting pan in a preheated oven at 400°F for 35–40 minutes, or until cooked through. Let cool, remove the meat from the bones, and cut into small cubes.

3 Heat the oil in a wok and fry the leek, garlic, and ginger for 3 minutes. Mix with the duck meat.

4 Sift the flour into a large bowl. Mix the yeast, sugar, and water in a separate bowl and leave in a warm place for 15 minutes. Pour the yeast mixture into the flour, together with the warm milk, mixing to form a firm dough.

5 Knead the dough on a floured surface for 5 minutes. Roll into

a sausage shape, 1 inch in diameter. Cut into 16 pieces, cover, and let stand for 20–25 minutes.

6 Flatten the dough pieces into 4-inch rounds. Place a spoonful of filling in the center of each, draw up the sides to form a "moneybag," and twist to seal.

7 Place the dumplings on a clean dish cloth in the base of a steamer, cover, and steam for 20 minutes.

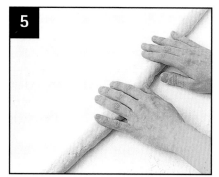

Spinach Meatballs

These are somewhat of a surprise! Balls of pork mixture are coated in spinach and steamed before being served with a sesame and soy sauce dip.

Serves 4

INGREDIENTS

4$^{1}/_{2}$ ounces pork
1 small egg
$^{1}/_{2}$-inch piece fresh ginger
   root, chopped
1 small onion, finely chopped
1 tbsp boiling water
2 tsp cornstarch
1 pound fresh spinach

2 tsp sesame seeds
1 ounce canned bamboo shoots,
   drained, rinsed, and chopped
2 slices smoked ham, chopped

SAUCE:
$^{2}/_{3}$ cup vegetable stock
$^{1}/_{2}$ tsp cornstarch

1 tsp cold water
1 tsp light soy sauce
$^{1}/_{2}$ tsp sesame oil
1 tbsp chopped chives

1 Grind the pork very finely in a food processor or meat grinder. Lightly beat the egg in a bowl and stir into the pork.

2 Put the ginger and onion in a separate bowl, add the boiling water, and let stand for 5 minutes. Drain and add to the pork mixture, together with the bamboo shoots, ham and cornstarch. Mix and roll into 12 balls between the palms of your hands.

3 Wash the spinach and remove the stalks. Blanch in boiling water for 10 seconds and drain well, pressing out as much moisture as possible. Slice the spinach into very thin strips, then mix with the sesame seeds. Spread out the mixture in a shallow baking pan. Roll the meatballs in the mixture to coat.

4 Place the meatballs on a heatproof plate in the base of

a steamer. Cover and steam for 8–10 minutes, until cooked through and tender.

5 Meanwhile, make the sauce. Put the stock in a saucepan and bring to a boil. Mix together the cornstarch and water to a smooth paste and stir it into the stock. Stir in the soy sauce, sesame oil, and chives. Transfer the cooked meatballs to a warm plate and serve with the sauce.

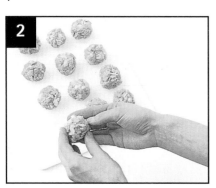

Steamed Cabbage Rolls

These small cabbage packets are quick and easy to prepare and cook. They are ideal for a speedy appetizer..

Serves 4

INGREDIENTS

8 cabbage leaves, trimmed
8 ounces skinless, boneless chicken
6 ounces peeled raw or
  cooked shrimp

1 tsp cornstarch
1/2 tsp chili powder
1 egg, lightly beaten
1 tbsp vegetable oil

1 leek, sliced
1 garlic clove, thinly sliced
sliced fresh red chili, to garnish

1 Bring a large saucepan of water to a boil. Blanch the cabbage leaves for 2 minutes. Drain, rinse under cold water, and drain again. Pat completely dry with paper towels and spread out on a counter.

2 Put the chicken and shrimp into a food processor and process until finely ground. Alternatively, grind them together in a meat grinder. Transfer the chicken mixture to a large bowl and add the cornstarch, chili powder, and egg, mixing together thoroughly.

3 Place 2 tablespoons of the chicken and shrimp mixture toward one end of each cabbage leaf. Fold the sides of the cabbage leaf around the filling and roll up to form a tight packet.

4 Arrange the packets, seam side down, in a single layer on a heatproof plate and cook in a steamer for 10 minutes, or until cooked through.

5 Meanwhile, heat the vegetable oil in a preheated wok. Add the leek and garlic and sauté for 1–2 minutes.

6 Transfer the cabbage packets to warmed individual serving plates and garnish with red chili slices. Serve with the leek and garlic sauté.

COOK'S TIP

Use Chinese cabbage or Savoy cabbage for this recipe, choosing leaves of a similar size for the packets.

Chinese Omelet

This is a fairly filling omelet, as it contains chicken and shrimp.
It is cooked as a whole omelet and then sliced for serving.

Serves 4

INGREDIENTS

8 eggs	12 jumbo shrimp, peeled and	2 tsp light soy sauce
2 cups cooked chicken, shredded	deveined	dash of chili sauce
	2 tbsp chopped chives	2 tbsp vegetable oil

1 Lightly beat the eggs in a large mixing bowl.

2 Add the shredded chicken and jumbo shrimp to the eggs, mixing well.

3 Stir in the chopped chives, soy sauce, and chili sauce, mixing well.

4 Heat the oil in a large skillet over a medium heat and add the egg mixture, tilting the skillet to coat the base completely. Cook over a medium heat, gently stirring the omelet with a fork occasionally, until the surface is just set and the underside is a golden brown color.

5 When the omelet is set, slide it out of the skillet with a spatula.

6 Cut the omelet into squares or slices to serve.

VARIATION

You could add extra flavor to the omelet by stirring in 3 tablespoons finely chopped fresh cilantro or 1 teaspoon sesame seeds with the chives in step 3.

COOK'S TIP

Add peas or other vegetables to the omelet and serve as a main course for 2 people.

Main Courses

This comprehensive chapter covers many cooking methods and ingredients to give a very wide variety of main meals for all occasions, be it a simple supper, a dinner party, or informal gathering. Fish, seafood, pork, lamb, beef, duck, and chicken are all used to their full potential to delight the palate.

When choosing ingredients, try to purchase them as fresh as possible, particularly fish and seafood. You can vary the meat and fish used to suit your personal preferences, as they are very adaptable recipes.

When entertaining, choose several different dishes to give as much variety of taste as possible, and prepare as much as you can in advance to enable you to spend more time with your guests than in the kitchen.

The portions in the recipes contained in this chapter are geared toward the traditional Chinese menu, and may be slightly smaller than a Western serving, so why not choose a selection and create your very own Chinese banquet!

Steamed Fish with Black Bean Sauce

The Chinese use a lot of whole fish in their cooking, and steaming is one of their preferred methods. It helps maintain both the flavor and the texture.

Serves 4

INGREDIENTS

2 pounds whole snapper, cleaned and
   scaled
3 garlic cloves, crushed
2 tbsp black bean sauce
1 tsp cornstarch

2 tsp sesame oil
2 tbsp light soy sauce
2 tsp superfine sugar
2 tbsp Chinese rice wine or
   dry sherry
1 small leek, shredded

1 small red bell pepper, seeded and
   cut into thin strips
shredded leek and lemon wedges,
   to garnish
boiled rice or noodles, to serve

1 Rinse the fish inside and out with cold running water and pat dry with paper towels. Make 2-3 diagonal slashes in the flesh on each side of the fish, using a sharp knife. Rub the garlic into the fish.

2 Thoroughly mix the black bean sauce, cornstarch, sesame oil, light soy sauce, sugar, and Chinese rice wine or dry sherry together in a bowl. Place the fish in a shallow heatproof dish and pour the sauce mixture over the top.

3 Sprinkle the leek and bell pepper strips on top of the sauce. Place the dish in the top of a steamer, cover, and steam for 10 minutes, or until the fish is cooked through. Transfer to a serving dish, garnish with shredded leek and lemon wedges, and serve with rice or noodles.

VARIATION

Whole sea bream or sea bass may be used in this recipe instead of snapper, if desired.

COOK'S TIP

Insert the point of a sharp knife into the fish to test if it is cooked. The fish is cooked through if the knife goes into the flesh easily.

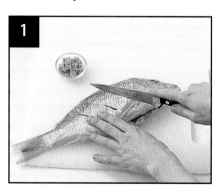

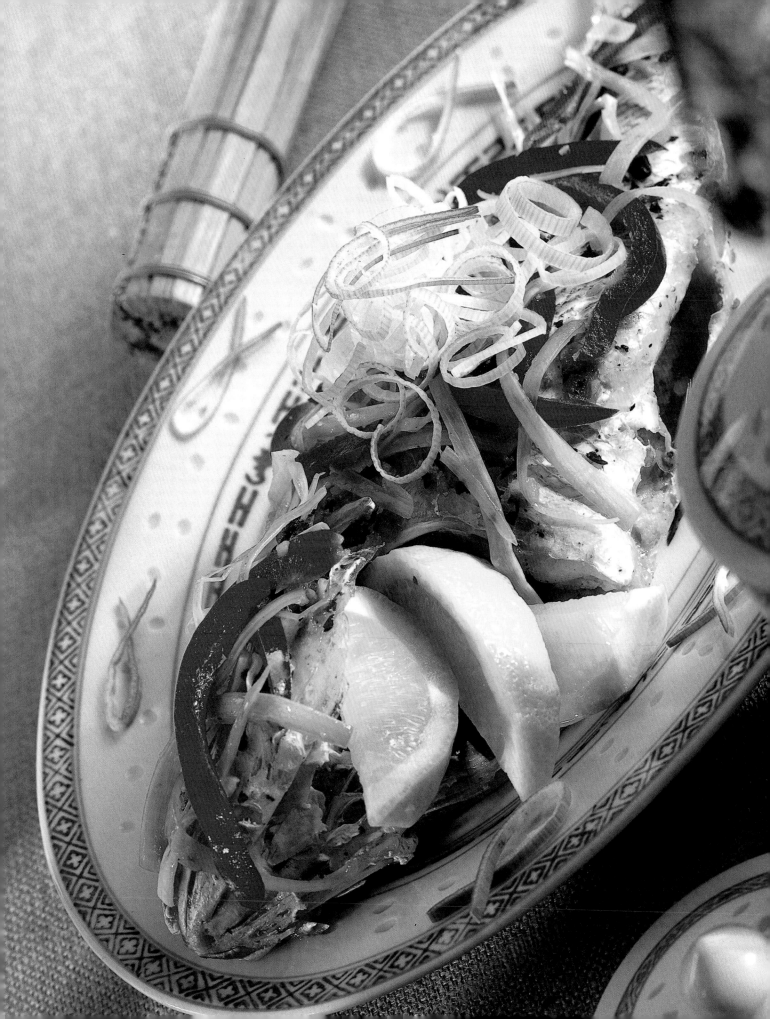

Steamed Snapper with Fruit & Ginger Stuffing

Red mullet may be used instead of the whole snapper, although they are a little more difficult to stuff because of their size. Use one mullet per person.

Serves 4

INGREDIENTS

3 pounds whole snapper, cleaned
    and scaled
6 ounces fresh spinach
orange slices and shredded scallion,
    to garnish

STUFFING:
2 cups cooked long grain rice
1 tsp grated fresh ginger root
2 scallions, finely chopped
2 tsp light soy sauce
1 tsp sesame oil

$1/2$ tsp ground star anise
1 orange, segmented and chopped

1 Rinse the fish inside and out under cold running water and pat dry with paper towels. Blanch the spinach for 40 seconds, rinse in cold water, and drain well, pressing out as much moisture as possible. Arrange the spinach on a heatproof plate and place the fish on top.

2 To make the stuffing, mix together the cooked rice, grated ginger, scallion, soy sauce, sesame oil, star anise and orange in a bowl.

3 Spoon the stuffing into the body cavity of the fish, pressing it in well with a spoon.

4 Cover the plate and cook in a steamer for 10 minutes, or until the fish is cooked through. Carefully transfer the fish to a warm serving dish, garnish with orange slices and shredded scallion, and serve immediately.

COOK'S TIP

The name snapper covers a family of tropical and subtropical fish that vary in color. They may be red, orange, pink, red, gray, or blue-green. Some are striped or spotted and they range in size from about 6 inches to 3 feet.

Trout with Pineapple

Pineapple is widely used in Chinese cooking. The tartness of fresh pineapple complements fish particularly well.

Serves 4

INGREDIENTS

4 trout fillets, skinned
2 tbsp vegetable oil
2 garlic cloves, cut into slivers
4 slices fresh pineapple, peeled
   and diced

1 celery stalk, sliced
1 tbsp light soy sauce
$^1/_4$ cup fresh or unsweetened
   pineapple juice
$^2/_3$ cup fish stock

1 tsp cornstarch
2 tsp water
shredded celery leaves and fresh red
   chili strips, to garnish

1 Cut the trout fillets into strips. Heat 1 tablespoon of the vegetable oil in a preheated wok until almost smoking. Reduce the heat slightly, add the fish, and sauté for 2 minutes. Remove from the wok and set aside.

2 Add the remaining oil to the wok, reduce the heat, and add the garlic, pineapple, and celery. Stir-fry for 1–2 minutes.

3 Add the soy sauce, pineapple juice, and fish stock to the wok. Bring to a boil and cook,

stirring, for 2–3 minutes, or until the sauce has reduced.

4 Blend the cornstarch with the water to form a smooth paste and stir it into the wok. Bring the sauce to a boil and cook, stirring constantly, until the sauce has thickened and cleared.

5 Return the fish to the wok, and cook, stirring gently, until heated through. Transfer to a warm serving dish and serve, garnished with shredded celery leaves and red chili strips.

COOK'S TIP

Use canned pineapple instead of fresh pineapple if desired, choosing slices in unsweetened, natural juice instead of syrup.

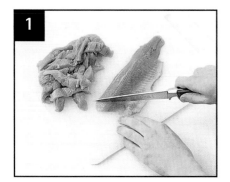

Mullet with Ginger

Ginger is used widely in Chinese cooking for its strong, pungent flavor. Always use fresh ginger when possible, but ground ginger may be used as an alternative when fresh is unavailable.

Serves 4

INGREDIENTS

1 whole mullet, cleaned and scaled
2 scallions, chopped
1 tsp grated fresh ginger root
1/2 cup garlic wine vinegar
1/2 cup light soy sauce
3 tsp superfine sugar

dash of chili sauce
1/2 cup fish stock
1 green bell pepper, seeded and
  thinly sliced

1 large tomato, peeled, seeded, and
  cut into thin strips
salt and pepper
sliced tomato, to garnish

1 Rinse the fish inside and out and pat thoroughly dry with paper towels.

2 Make 3 diagonal slits in the flesh on each side of the fish. Season with salt and pepper inside and out.

3 Place the fish on a heatproof plate and scatter the chopped scallions and grated ginger over the top. Cover and steam for 10 minutes, or until the fish is cooked through.

4 Meanwhile, place the garlic wine vinegar, soy sauce, sugar, chili sauce, fish stock, bell pepper, and tomato in a saucepan and bring to a boil, stirring occasionally. Cook over a high heat until the sauce has slightly reduced and thickened.

5 Remove the fish from the steamer and transfer to a warm serving dish. Pour the sauce over the fish, garnish with tomato slices, and serve immediately.

COOK'S TIP

Use fillets of fish for this recipe if desired, and reduce the cooking time to 5–7 minutes.

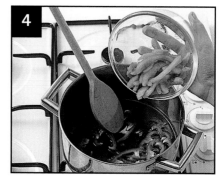

Szechuan White Fish

*Szechuan pepper is quite hot and should be used sparingly
to avoid making the dish unbearably spicy.*

Serves 4

INGREDIENTS

12 ounces white fish fillets
1 small egg, beaten
3 tbsp all-purpose flour
4 tbsp dry white wine
3 tbsp light soy sauce
vegetable oil, for frying
1 garlic clove, cut into slivers

$\frac{1}{2}$-inch piece fresh ginger root,
   finely chopped
1 onion, finely chopped
1 celery stalk, chopped
1 fresh red chili, chopped
3 scallions, chopped
1 tsp rice wine vinegar

$\frac{1}{2}$ tsp ground Szechuan pepper
$\frac{3}{4}$ cup fish stock
1 tsp superfine sugar
1 tsp cornstarch
2 tsp water
chili flowers and celery leaves,
   to garnish

1 Cut the fish fillets into
1$\frac{1}{2}$-inch cubes.

2 In a mixing bowl, beat
together the egg, flour, wine,
and 1 tablespoon of soy sauce to
make a batter.

3 Dip the cubes of fish into the
batter to coat well.

4 Heat the oil in a preheated
wok until it is almost
smoking. Reduce the heat slightly

and cook the fish, in batches, for
2–3 minutes, until golden brown.
Drain on paper towels, set aside,
and keep warm.

5 Carefully pour all but 1
tablespoon of the oil from the
wok and return to the heat. Add
the garlic, ginger, onion, celery,
chili, and scallions and stir-fry for
1–2 minutes.

6 Stir in the remaining soy
sauce and the vinegar.

7 Add the Szechuan pepper, fish
stock, and sugar to the wok.
Blend the cornstarch with the
water to form a smooth paste and
stir it into the stock. Bring to a boil
and cook, stirring, for 1 minute,
until the sauce thickens and clears.

8 Return the fish to the wok
and cook for 1–2 minutes,
until thoroughly heated through.
Transfer to a serving dish, garnish
with chili flowers and celery
leaves, and serve.

Crispy Fish

This is a very hot dish—not for the fainthearted! It may be made
without the chili flavorings, if desired.

Serves 4

INGREDIENTS

1 pound white fish fillets

BATTER:
1/2 cup all-purpose flour
1 egg, separated
1 tbsp peanut oil

4 tbsp milk
vegetable oil, for deep-frying

SAUCE:
1 fresh red chili, chopped
2 garlic cloves, crushed
pinch of chili powder

3 tbsp tomato paste
1 tbsp rice wine vinegar
2 tbsp dark soy sauce
2 tbsp Chinese rice wine
2 tbsp water
pinch of superfine sugar

1 Cut the fish into 1-inch cubes and set aside. Sift the flour into a mixing bowl and make a well in the center. Add the egg yolk and oil to the bowl and gradually stir in the milk, incorporating the flour to form a smooth batter. Let stand for 20 minutes.

2 Beat the egg white until it forms peaks, and fold it into the batter. Heat the oil in a preheated wok. Dip the fish into the batter and fry, in batches, for 8–10 minutes, until cooked through. Remove the fish from the wok with a slotted spoon, set aside, and keep warm.

3 Pour off all but 1 tablespoon of oil from the wok and return to the heat. Add the chili, garlic, chili powder, tomato paste, rice wine vinegar, soy sauce, Chinese rice wine, water, and sugar and cook, stirring, for 3–4 minutes.

4 Return the fish to the wok and stir gently to coat it in the sauce. Cook for 2–3 minutes, until hot. Transfer the fish and sauce to a warm serving dish and serve immediately.

COOK'S TIP

Take care when pouring
hot oil from the wok and ensure
that you transfer it to a suitable
bowl until cool.

Seafood Medley

*Use any combination of fish and seafood in this delicious dish
of coated fish served in a wine sauce.*

Serves 4

INGREDIENTS

2 tbsp dry white wine
1 egg white, lightly beaten
$^1/_2$ tsp Chinese five-spice powder
1 tsp cornstarch
$10^1/_2$ ounces raw shrimp, peeled and deveined

$4^1/_2$ ounces prepared squid, cut into rings
$4^1/_2$ ounces white fish fillets, cut into strips
vegetable oil, for deep-frying

1 green bell pepper, seeded and cut into thin strips
1 carrot, peeled and cut into thin strips
4 baby corncobs, halved lengthwise

1 Mix together the wine, egg white, Chinese five-spice powder, and cornstarch in a large bowl, combining well. Add the shrimp, squid rings, and fish fillets and stir gently to coat thoroughly and evenly. Remove the fish and seafood with a slotted spoon, reserving any leftover wine and cornstarch mixture.

2 Heat the oil in a preheated wok. Add the shrimp, squid, and fish strips and deep-fry for 2–3 minutes. Remove the seafood mixture from the wok with a slotted spoon and set aside.

3 Pour off all but 1 tablespoon of oil from the wok and return to the heat. Add the bell pepper, carrot, and corncobs and stir-fry for 4–5 minutes.

4 Return the seafood mixture to the wok and add any remaining wine and cornstarch mixture. Cook, stirring well to heat through. Transfer to a serving plate and serve immediately.

COOK'S TIP

Open up the squid rings and, using a sharp knife, score a lattice pattern on the flesh to make them look attractive.

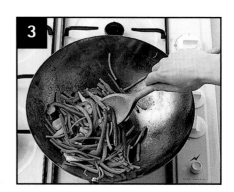

Fried Shrimp with Cashews

Cashew nuts are delicious as part of a stir-fry with almost any other ingredient.
Use the unsalted variety in cooking.

Serves 4

INGREDIENTS

2 garlic cloves, crushed
1 tbsp cornstarch
pinch of superfine sugar
1 pound raw jumbo shrimp
4 tbsp vegetable oil
1 leek, sliced

4¹/₂ ounces broccoli florets
1 orange bell pepper, seeded
  and diced
³/₄ cup unsalted cashew nuts

SAUCE:
³/₄ cup fish stock
1 tbsp cornstarch
dash of chili sauce
2 tsp sesame oil
1 tbsp Chinese rice wine

1 Mix together the garlic, cornstarch, and sugar in a large bowl. Peel and devein the jumbo shrimp. Stir the shrimp into the cornstarch mixture to coat thoroughly.

2 Heat the oil in a preheated wok and add the shrimp mixture. Stir-fry over a high heat for 20–30 seconds, until the shrimp turn pink. Remove the shrimp from the wok with a slotted spoon, drain on paper towels, and set aside.

3 Add the leek, broccoli, and bell pepper to the wok and stir-fry for 2 minutes.

4 To make the sauce, mix together the fish stock, cornstarch, chili sauce to taste, the sesame oil, and Chinese rice wine. Add the mixture to the wok, together with the cashews. Return the shrimp to the wok and cook, stirring frequently, for 1 minute to heat through completely. Transfer to a warm serving dish and serve immediately.

VARIATION

This recipe also works well with chicken, pork, or beef strips instead of the shrimp. Use 8 ounces meat instead of 1 pound shrimp.

Shrimp Fu Yong

The classic ingredients of this popular dish are eggs, carrots, and small shrimp.
Add extra ingredients, such as peas or crab meat, if desired.

Serves 4

INGREDIENTS

2 tbsp vegetable oil
1 carrot, peeled and grated
5 eggs, beaten

8 ounces raw small shrimp, peeled
1 tbsp light soy sauce
pinch of Chinese five-spice powder

2 scallions, chopped
2 tsp sesame seeds
1 tsp sesame oil

1 Heat the vegetable oil in a preheated wok.

2 Add the carrot and stir-fry for 1–2 minutes.

3 Push the carrot to one side of the wok and add the eggs. Cook, stirring gently, for 1–2 minutes.

4 Stir the small shrimp, soy sauce, and five-spice powder into the mixture in the wok. Stir-fry the mixture for 2–3 minutes, or until the small shrimp have changed color and the mixture is almost dry.

5 Turn the shrimp fu yong out onto a warm serving plate and sprinkle the scallions, sesame seeds, and sesame oil on top. Serve immediately.

VARIATION

For a more substantial dish, you could add 1 cup cooked long-grain rice with the small shrimp in step 4. Taste and adjust the quantities of soy sauce, Chinese five-spice powder, and sesame oil if necessary. This is a useful way of using up leftover rice.

COOK'S TIP

If only cooked shrimp are available, add them just before the end of cooking, but make sure they are fully incorporated into the fu yong. They require only heating through. Overcooking will make them chewy and tasteless.

Cantonese Shrimp

This shrimp dish is very simple and is ideal for supper or lunch when time is short.

Serves 4

INGREDIENTS

5 tbsp vegetable oil
4 garlic cloves, crushed
1¹/₂ pounds raw shrimp, shelled and
   deveined
2-inch piece fresh ginger root,
   chopped

6 ounces lean pork, diced
1 leek, sliced
3 eggs, beaten
shredded leek and red bell pepper
   matchsticks, to garnish

SAUCE:
2 tbsp dry sherry
2 tbsp light soy sauce
2 tsp superfine sugar
²/₃ cup fish stock
4¹/₂ tsp cornstarch
3 tbsp water

1 Heat 2 tablespoons of the vegetable oil in a preheated wok. Add the garlic and stir-fry for about 30 seconds. Add the shrimp and stir-fry for 5 minutes, or until they change color. Remove the shrimp from the wok with a slotted spoon, drain, set aside, and keep warm.

2 Add the remaining oil to the wok and heat. Add the ginger, diced pork, and leek and stir-fry over a medium heat for 4-5 minutes, or until the pork is lightly colored and sealed.

3 Add the sherry, soy sauce, sugar, and fish stock to the wok. Blend the cornstarch with the water to form a smooth paste and stir it into the wok. Cook, stirring, until the sauce thickens and clears.

4 Return the shrimp to the wok and add the beaten eggs. Cook for 5–6 minutes, stirring occasionally, until the eggs set. Transfer to a warm serving dish, garnish with shredded leek and bell pepper matchsticks, and serve.

COOK'S TIP

If possible, use Chinese rice wine instead of the sherry.

Squid With Oyster Sauce

Squid is a delicious fish that, contrary to popular belief, is not rubbery. If prepared and cooked correctly, it is a quick cooking, attractive, and tasty ingredient.

Serves 4

INGREDIENTS

1 pound squid
²/₃ cup vegetable oil
¹/₂-inch piece fresh ginger
   root, grated

2 ounces snow peas
5 tbsp hot fish stock
red bell pepper triangles, to garnish

SAUCE:
1 tbsp oyster sauce
1 tbsp light soy sauce
pinch of superfine sugar
1 garlic clove, crushed

1 To prepare the squid, cut down the center of the body lengthwise. Flatten the squid out, inside uppermost, and score a lattice design deep into the flesh, using a sharp knife.

2 To make the sauce, combine the oyster sauce, soy sauce, sugar, and garlic in a small bowl. Stir to dissolve the sugar and set aside until required.

3 Heat the vegetable oil in a preheated wok until almost smoking. Lower the heat slightly,

add the squid, and stir-fry until they curl up. Remove with a slotted spoon and drain thoroughly on paper towels.

4 Pour off all but 2 tablespoons of the oil and return the wok to the heat. Add the ginger and snow peas and stir-fry for about 1 minute.

5 Return the squid to the wok and pour in the sauce and hot fish stock. Simmer the mixture for about 3 minutes, or until the liquid has thickened.

6 Transfer to a warm serving dish, garnish with bell pepper triangles, and serve immediately.

COOK'S TIP

Take care not to overcook the squid, otherwise it will be rubbery and unappetizing.

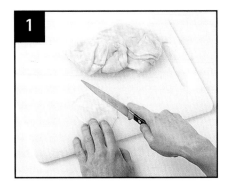

Scallops In Ginger Sauce

Scallops are both attractive and delicious and make this a special dish. Cooked with ginger and orange, this dish is perfect served with plain rice.

Serves 4

INGREDIENTS

2 tbsp vegetable oil
1 pound scallops, cleaned
 and halved
1-inch piece fresh ginger root,
 finely chopped

3 garlic cloves, crushed
2 leeks, shredded
$^3/_4$ cup shelled peas
$4^1/_2$ ounces canned bamboo shoots,
 drained and rinsed

2 tbsp light soy sauce
2 tbsp unsweetened orange juice
1 tsp superfine sugar
orange zest, to garnish

1 Heat the oil in a preheated wok. Add the scallops and stir-fry for 1–2 minutes. Remove the scallops from the wok with a slotted spoon and set aside.

2 Add the ginger and garlic to the wok and stir-fry for 30 seconds. Stir in the leeks and peas and cook, stirring, for a further 2 minutes.

3 Add the bamboo shoots and return the scallops to the wok. Stir gently to mix without breaking up the scallops.

4 Stir in the soy sauce, orange juice, and sugar and cook for 1–2 minutes. Transfer to a serving dish, garnish with the orange zest, and serve immediately.

COOK'S TIP

The edible parts of a scallop are the round white muscle and the orange and white coral or roe. The frilly skirt surrounding the muscle—the gills and mantle—may be used for making shellfish stock. All other parts should be discarded.

COOK'S TIP

Frozen scallops may be thawed and used in this recipe, adding them at the end of cooking to prevent them from breaking up. If you are buying scallops already shelled, check whether they are fresh or frozen. Fresh scallops are cream colored and more translucent, while frozen scallops tend to be pure white.

Crab in Ginger Sauce

*In this recipe, the crabs are served in the shell for ease and visual effect
and coated in a glossy ginger sauce.*

Serves 4

INGREDIENTS

2 small cooked crabs
2 tbsp vegetable oil
3-inch piece fresh ginger root,
    grated
2 garlic cloves, thinly sliced

1 green bell pepper, seeded and cut
    into thin strips
6 scallions, cut into 1-inch lengths
2 tbsp dry sherry

$^1/_2$ tsp sesame oil
$^2/_3$ cup fish stock
1 tsp light brown sugar
2 tsp cornstarch
$^2/_3$ cup water

1 Rinse the crabs and gently
loosen around the shell at the
top. Using a sharp knife, cut away
the gray tissue and discard. Rinse
the crabs again.

2 Twist off the legs and claws
from the crabs. Using a pair
of crab claw crackers or a cleaver,
gently crack the claws to break
through the shell to expose the
flesh. Remove and discard any
loose pieces of shell.

3 Separate the body and discard
the inedible lungs and sac.

Cut down the center of each crab
to separate the body into two
pieces and then cut each of these
in half again.

4 Heat the oil in a preheated
wok. Add the ginger and
garlic and stir-fry for 1 minute.
Add the crab pieces and stir-fry for
1 minute.

5 Stir in the bell pepper,
scallions, sherry, sesame oil,
stock, and sugar. Bring to a boil,
reduce the heat, cover, and simmer
for 3–4 minutes.

6 Blend the cornstarch with
the water to make a smooth
paste and stir it into the wok.
Bring to a boil, stirring, until the
sauce is thickened and clear.
Transfer to a warm serving dish
and serve immediately.

COOK'S TIP

*If desired, remove
the crab meat from
the shells prior to
stir-frying and add to the wok with
the bell pepper.*

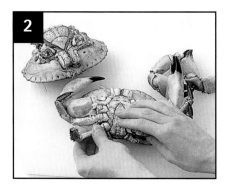

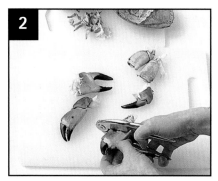

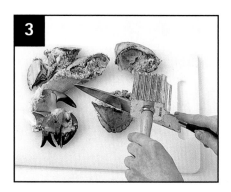

Chili Chicken

This is quite a hot dish, using fresh chilies. If you prefer
a milder dish, halve the number of chilies used.

Serves 4

INGREDIENTS

12 ounces skinless, boneless
   lean chicken
$^1/_2$ tsp salt
1 egg white, lightly beaten
2 tbsp cornstarch
4 tbsp vegetable oil

2 garlic cloves, crushed
$^1/_2$-inch piece fresh ginger
   root, grated
1 red bell pepper, seeded and diced
1 green bell pepper, seeded
   and diced

2 fresh red chilies, chopped
2 tbsp light soy sauce
1 tbsp dry sherry or Chinese rice wine
1 tbsp wine vinegar

1 Cut the chicken into cubes
and place in a mixing bowl.
Add the salt, egg white,
cornstarch, and 1 tablespoon of
the oil. Turn the chicken in the
mixture to coat thoroughly.

2 Heat the remaining oil in a
preheated wok. Add the garlic
and ginger and stir-fry for
30 seconds.

3 Add the chicken pieces to
the wok and stir-fry for
2–3 minutes, or until browned.

4 Stir in the bell peppers,
chilies, soy sauce, sherry or
Chinese rice wine, and wine
vinegar and cook for a further
2–3 minutes, until the chicken is
cooked through. Transfer to a
warm serving dish and serve.

VARIATION

This recipe works well if you use
12 ounces lean steak, cut into thin
strips, or 1 pound raw shrimp,
instead of the chicken.

COOK'S TIP

When preparing chilies,
wear protective gloves
to prevent the juices from
burning and irritating your hands.
Be careful not to touch your face,
especially your lips or eyes, until
you have washed your hands.

Lemon Chicken

This is on everyone's list of favorite Chinese dishes, and it is so simple to make. Fried chicken is cooked in a tangy lemon sauce in minutes and is great served with stir-fried vegetables.

Serves 4

INGREDIENTS

vegetable oil, for deep-frying
1¹/₂ pounds skinless, boneless
   chicken, cut into strips
lemon slices and shredded scallion,
   to garnish

SAUCE:
1 tbsp cornstarch
6 tbsp cold water
3 tbsp fresh lemon juice

2 tbsp sweet sherry
¹/₂ tsp superfine sugar

1 Heat the oil in a preheated wok until almost smoking. Reduce the heat and stir-fry the chicken strips for 3–4 minutes, until cooked through. Remove the chicken with a slotted spoon, set aside, and keep warm. Drain the oil from the wok.

2 To make the sauce, mix the cornstarch with 2 tablespoons of the water to form a paste.

3 Pour the lemon juice and remaining water into the wok. Add the sherry and sugar and bring to a boil, stirring until the sugar has completely dissolved.

4 Stir in the cornstarch mixture and return to a boil. Reduce the heat and simmer, stirring constantly, for about 2-3 minutes, until the sauce is thickened and clear.

5 Transfer the chicken strips to a warm serving plate and pour the lemon sauce over the top. Garnish with the lemon slices and shredded scallion and serve immediately.

COOK'S TIP

If you would prefer to use chicken portions rather than strips, cook them in the oil, covered, over a low heat for about 30 minutes, or until cooked through.

Braised Chicken

This is a delicious way to cook a whole chicken. It has a wonderful glaze, which is served as a sauce.

Serves 4

INGREDIENTS

3 pounds 5 ounces whole chicken
3 tbsp vegetable oil
1 tbsp peanut oil
2 tbsp dark brown sugar

5 tbsp dark soy sauce
$^{2}/_{3}$ cup water
2 garlic cloves, crushed
1 small onion, chopped

1 fresh red chili, chopped
celery leaves and chives, to garnish

1 Thoroughly clean the chicken inside and out with damp paper towels.

2 Put the oil in a large wok, add the sugar, and heat gently until the sugar caramelizes. Stir in the soy sauce. Add the chicken and turn it in the mixture to coat thoroughly on all sides.

3 Add the water, garlic, onion, and chili. Cover and simmer, turning the chicken occasionally, for about 1 hour, or until cooked through. Test by piercing a thigh with the point of a sharp knife—the juices will run clear when the chicken is cooked.

4 Remove the chicken from the wok and set aside. Increase the heat and reduce the sauce in the wok until thickened. Cut the chicken into portions, garnish with celery leaves and chives, and serve with the sauce.

COOK'S TIP

When caramelizing the sugar, do not turn the heat too high, otherwise it may burn.

VARIATION

For a spicier sauce, add 1 tbsp finely chopped fresh ginger root and 1 tbsp ground Szechuan peppercorns with the chili in step 3. If the flavor of dark soy sauce is too strong for your taste, substitute 2 tbsp dark soy sauce and 3 tbsp light soy sauce. This will result in a more delicate taste without sacrificing the attractive color of the dish.

Chicken With Cashews & Vegetables

This is a popular dish in Chinese restaurants in the West, although nothing beats making it yourself.

Serves 4

INGREDIENTS

10 $^1/_2$ ounces boneless, skinless
   chicken breasts
1 tbsp cornstarch
1 tsp sesame oil
1 tbsp hoisin sauce
1 tsp light soy sauce
3 garlic cloves, crushed

2 tbsp vegetable oil
$^3/_4$ cup unsalted cashews
1 ounce snow peas
1 celery stalk, sliced
1 onion, cut into 8 pieces
2 ounces bean sprouts
1 red bell pepper, seeded and diced

SAUCE:
2 tsp cornstarch
2 tbsp hoisin sauce
1 cup chicken stock

1 Trim any fat from the chicken breasts and cut the meat into thin strips. Place the chicken in a large mixing bowl. Sprinkle with the cornstarch and toss to coat the chicken strips in it, shaking off any excess. Mix together the sesame oil, hoisin sauce, soy sauce, and 1 crushed garlic clove. Pour this mixture over the chicken, turning to coat thoroughly. Marinate for 20 minutes.

2 Heat half the vegetable oil in a preheated wok. Add the cashews and stir-fry for 1 minute, until browned. Add the snow peas, celery, the remaining garlic, the onion, bean sprouts, and red bell pepper and cook, stirring occasionally, for 2–3 minutes. Remove all the vegetables from the wok with a slotted spoon, drain, set aside, and keep warm.

3 Heat the remaining oil in the wok. Remove the chicken from the marinade and stir-fry for 3–4 minutes. Return the vegetables to the wok.

4 To make the sauce, mix the cornstarch, hoisin sauce, and chicken stock together and pour into the wok. Bring to a boil, stirring until thickened and clear. Serve immediately.

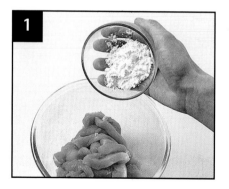
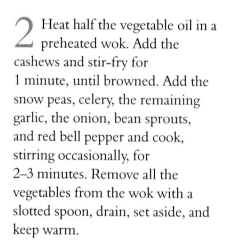

Chicken Chop Suey

Well-known and popular, chop suey dishes are easy to make and delicious. They are based on bean sprouts and soy sauce with a meat or vegetable flavoring.

Serves 4

INGREDIENTS

4 tbsp light soy sauce
2 tsp light brown sugar
1¼ pounds skinless, boneless
  chicken breasts
3 tbsp vegetable oil

2 onions, quartered
2 garlic cloves, crushed
12 ounces bean sprouts
1 tbsp sesame oil

1 tbsp cornstarch
3 tbsp water
2 cups chicken stock
shredded leek, to garnish

1 Mix the soy sauce and sugar together, stirring until the sugar has dissolved.

2 Trim any fat from the chicken and cut the meat into thin strips. Place the chicken strips in a shallow glass dish and spoon the soy mixture over them, turning to coat. Marinate in the refrigerator for 20 minutes.

3 Heat the oil in a preheated wok. Add the chicken and stir-fry for 2–3 minutes, until golden brown.

4 Add the onions and garlic and cook for a further 2 minutes. Add the bean sprouts, cook for a further 4–5 minutes, then add the sesame oil.

5 Blend the cornstarch with the water to form a smooth paste. Pour the chicken stock into the wok, together with the cornstarch paste, and bring the mixture to a boil, stirring constantly until the sauce is thickened and clear. Transfer to a warm serving dish, garnish with shredded leek, and serve immediately.

VARIATION

This recipe may be made with strips of lean steak, pork, or with mixed vegetables. Change the type of stock accordingly.

Chicken with Yellow Bean Sauce

Ready-made yellow bean sauce is available from large supermarkets and Chinese grocery stores.
It is made from yellow soy beans and is quite salty in flavor.

Serves 4

INGREDIENTS

1 pound skinless, boneless
   chicken breasts
1 egg white, beaten
1 tbsp cornstarch
1 tbsp rice wine vinegar
1 tbsp light soy sauce

1 tsp superfine sugar
3 tbsp vegetable oil
1 garlic clove, crushed
1/2-inch piece fresh ginger
   root, grated

1 green bell pepper, seeded
   and diced
2 large mushrooms, sliced
3 tbsp yellow bean sauce
yellow or green bell pepper strips,
   to garnish

1 Trim any fat from the chicken and cut the meat into 1-inch cubes.

2 Mix the egg white and cornstarch in a shallow bowl. Add the chicken and turn in the mixture to coat. Set aside for 20 minutes.

3 Mix the vinegar, soy sauce, and sugar in a bowl.

4 Remove the chicken from the egg white mixture.

5 Heat the oil in a preheated wok, add the chicken, and stir-fry for 3–4 minutes, until golden brown. Remove the chicken from the wok with a slotted spoon, set aside, and keep warm.

6 Stir-fry the garlic, ginger, bell pepper, and mushrooms for 1–2 minutes.

7 Add the yellow bean sauce and cook for 1 minute. Stir in the vinegar mixture and return the chicken to the wok. Cook for

1–2 minutes and serve hot, garnished with bell pepper strips.

VARIATION

Black bean sauce would work equally well with this recipe. Although this would affect the appearance of the dish, as it is much darker in color, the flavors would be compatible.

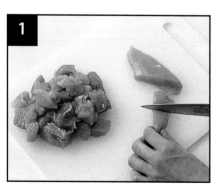

Crispy Chicken

In this recipe, the chicken is brushed with a syrup and deep-fried until golden.
It is a little time-consuming, but well worth the effort.

Serves 4

INGREDIENTS

3 pounds 5 ounces whole chicken
2 tbsp clear honey

2 tsp Chinese five-spice powder
2 tbsp rice wine vinegar

3 ³/₄ cups vegetable oil, for frying
chili sauce, to serve

1 Rinse the chicken inside and out under cold running water and pat dry with paper towels.

2 Bring a large saucepan of water to a boil and remove from the heat. Place the chicken in the water, cover, and set aside for 20 minutes. Remove the chicken from the water and pat dry with paper towels. Cool and chill in the refrigerator for 8 hours or overnight.

3 To make the glaze, mix together the clear honey, Chinese five-spice powder, and rice wine vinegar.

4 Brush some of the glaze all over the chicken and return to the refrigerator for 20 minutes. Repeat this process until all the glaze has been used up. Return the chicken to the refrigerator for at least 2 hours after the final coating.

5 Using a cleaver or heavy kitchen knife, open the chicken out by splitting it through the center through the breast, and then cut each half into 4 pieces.

6 Heat the oil for deep-frying in a wok until almost smoking. Reduce the heat and fry each piece of chicken for 5–7 minutes, until golden and cooked through. Remove from the oil with a slotted spoon and drain on absorbent paper towels.

7 Transfer to a warm serving dish and serve hot with a little chili sauce.

COOK'S TIP

If it is easier, use chicken portions instead of a whole chicken. You could also use chicken legs for this recipe, if desired.

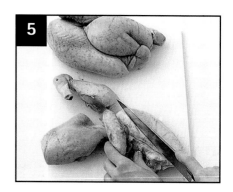

Spicy Peanut Chicken

This quick dish has many variations, but this version includes the classic combination of peanuts, chicken, and chilies, blending together to give a wonderfully flavored dish.

Serves 4

INGREDIENTS

10$^1/_2$ ounces skinless, boneless
   chicken breast
2 tbsp peanut oil
1 cup unsalted peanuts
1 fresh red chili, sliced
1 green bell pepper, seeded and cut
   into strips

1 tsp sesame oil
fried rice, to serve

SAUCE:
$^2/_3$ cup chicken stock
1 tbsp Chinese rice wine or
   dry sherry

1 tbsp light soy sauce
1$^1/_2$ tsp light brown sugar
2 garlic cloves, crushed
1 tsp grated fresh ginger root
1 tsp rice wine vinegar

1 Trim any fat from the chicken and cut the meat into 1-inch cubes. Set aside.

2 Heat the peanut oil in a preheated wok. Add the peanuts and stir-fry for 1 minute. Remove the peanuts with a slotted spoon and set aside.

3 Add the chicken to the wok and cook for 1–2 minutes. Stir in the chili and green bell pepper and cook for 1 minute.

Remove from the wok with a slotted spoon and set aside.

4 Put half the peanuts in a food processor and process until almost smooth. Alternatively, place them in a plastic bag and crush them with a rolling pin.

5 To make the sauce, add the chicken stock, Chinese rice wine or dry sherry, soy sauce, sugar, garlic, ginger, and rice wine vinegar to the wok.

6 Heat the sauce gently and stir in the peanut purée, peanuts, chicken, chili, and bell pepper.

7 Sprinkle the sesame oil into the wok, stir, and cook for 1 minute. Serve hot with fried rice.

COOK'S TIP

If necessary, process the peanuts with a little of the stock in step 4 to form a softer paste.

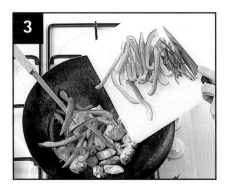

Chinese Chicken Salad

This is a refreshing dish suitable for a summer meal or light lunch.

Serves 4

INGREDIENTS

8 ounces skinless, boneless
    chicken breasts
2 tsp light soy sauce
1 tsp sesame oil
1 tsp sesame seeds
2 tbsp vegetable oil
4¹/₂ ounces bean sprouts

1 red bell pepper, seeded and
    thinly sliced
1 carrot, peeled and cut into
    matchsticks
3 baby corncobs, sliced
chives and carrot matchsticks, to
    garnish

SAUCE:
2 tsp rice wine vinegar
1 tbsp light soy sauce
dash of chili oil

1 Place the chicken in a shallow glass dish.

2 Mix together the soy sauce and sesame oil and pour the mixture over the chicken. Sprinkle with sesame seeds and let stand for 20 minutes.

3 Remove the chicken from the marinade and cut the meat into slices.

4 Heat the oil in a preheated wok. Add the chicken and fry for 4-5 minutes, until cooked through and golden brown on both sides. Remove the chicken from the wok with a slotted spoon, set aside, and let cool.

5 Add the bean sprouts, bell pepper, carrot, and baby corncobs to the wok and stir-fry for 2–3 minutes. Remove from the wok with a slotted spoon and cool.

6 To make the sauce, mix the rice wine vinegar, light soy sauce, and chili oil together.

7 Arrange the chicken and vegetables on a serving plate. Spoon the sauce over the salad, garnish with snipped chives and carrot matchsticks, and serve.

COOK'S TIP

If you have time, make the sauce and let stand for 30 minutes for the flavors to fully develop.

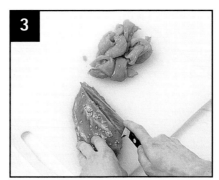

Peking Duck

No Chinese cookbook would be complete without this famous recipe. Crispy skinned duck is served with pancakes and a tangy sauce for a really special meal.

Serves 4

INGREDIENTS

4 pounds duck
7^1/$_2$ cups boiling water
4 tbsp clear honey
2 tsp dark soy sauce
2 tbsp sesame oil

^{1}/$_2$ cup hoisin sauce
^{2}/$_3$ cup superfine sugar
^{1}/$_2$ cup water

carrot strips, to garnish
Chinese pancakes, cucumber
   matchsticks, and scallions, to serve

1 Place the duck on a rack set over a roasting pan and pour 5 cups of the boiling water over it. Remove the duck and rack and discard the water. Pat dry with paper towels, replace the duck and the rack, and set aside for several hours.

2 Mix together the honey, remaining boiling water, and soy sauce. Brush the mixture over the skin and inside the duck. Reserve the remaining glaze. Set the duck aside for 1 hour, until the glaze has dried.

3 Coat the duck with another layer of glaze. Let dry and repeat until all the glaze is used.

4 Heat the oil and add the hoisin sauce, sugar, and water. Simmer for 2–3 minutes, until thickened. Cool and refrigerate.

5 Cook the duck in a preheated oven at 375°F for 30 minutes. Turn the duck over and cook for 20 minutes. Turn the duck again and cook for 20–30 minutes, or until cooked through and the skin is crisp.

6 Remove the duck from the oven and set aside for 10 minutes. Meanwhile, heat the pancakes in a steamer for 5–7 minutes. Cut the duck into strips, garnish with the carrot strips, and serve with the pancakes, sauce, cucumber matchsticks, and scallions.

COOK'S TIP

Keep the pancakes covered while working to prevent them from drying out.

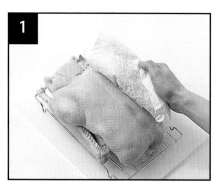

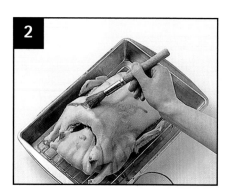

Duck In Spicy Sauce

Chinese five-spice powder gives a lovely flavor to this sliced duck,
and the chili adds a little subtle heat.

Serves 4

INGREDIENTS

1 tbsp vegetable oil
1 tsp grated fresh ginger root
1 garlic clove, crushed
1 fresh red chili, chopped
12 ounces skinless, boneless duck,
    cut into strips

$4^1/2$ ounces cauliflower, cut
    into florets
2 ounces snow peas
2 ounces baby corncobs,
    halved lengthwise
$1^1/4$ cups chicken stock
1 tsp Chinese five-spice powder

2 tsp Chinese rice wine or dry sherry
1 tsp cornstarch
2 tsp water
1 tsp sesame oil

1 Heat the vegetable oil in a preheated wok. Lower the heat slightly and add the ginger, garlic, chili, and duck and stir-fry for 2-3 minutes. Remove from the wok with a slotted spoon and set aside.

2 Add the cauliflower florets, snow peas, and baby corncobs to the wok and stir-fry for 2-3 minutes. Pour off any excess oil from the wok and push the vegetables to one side.

3 Return the duck to the wok and pour in the stock. Sprinkle the Chinese five-spice powder over the top, stir in the rice wine or sherry, and cook over a low heat for about 15 minutes, until the duck is tender.

4 Blend the cornstarch with the water to form a smooth paste and stir into the wok, together with the sesame oil. Bring to a boil, stirring until the sauce has thickened and cleared.

5 Transfer the duck and spicy sauce to a warm serving dish and serve immediately.

COOK'S TIP

Omit the chili for a milder dish, or seed the chili before adding it to remove some of the heat.

Honey-glazed Duck

This honey and soy glaze gives a wonderful sheen and flavor to the duck skin.
This is such a simple recipe, yet the result is delicious.

Serves 4

INGREDIENTS

1 tsp dark soy sauce
2 tbsp clear honey
1 tsp garlic vinegar
2 garlic cloves, crushed

1 tsp ground star anise
2 tsp cornstarch
2 tsp water

2 large boneless duck breasts, about
    8 ounces each
celery leaves, cucumber matchsticks,
    and snipped chives, to garnish

1 Mix together the soy sauce, clear honey, garlic vinegar, garlic, and star anise. Blend the cornstarch with the water to form a smooth paste and stir it into the mixture.

2 Place the duck breasts in a shallow ovenproof dish. Brush with the soy marinade, turning to coat them completely. Cover and marinate in the refrigerator for at least 2 hours, or overnight if possible.

3 Remove the duck from the marinade and cook in a preheated oven at 425°F for 20–25 minutes, basting frequently with the glaze.

4 Remove the duck from the oven and transfer to a preheated broiler. Broil for about 3–4 minutes to caramelize the top of the duck.

5 Remove the duck from the broiler pan and cut into thin slices. Arrange the duck slices in a warm serving dish, garnish with celery leaves, cucumber matchsticks, and snipped chives, and serve immediately.

COOK'S TIP

If the duck begins to burn slightly while it is cooking in the oven, cover with foil. To be sure the duck breasts are cooked through, insert the point of a sharp knife into the thickest part of the flesh. The juices should run clear.

Duck With Mangoes

Use fresh mangoes in this recipe for a terrific flavor and color.
If they are unavailable, use canned mangoes and rinse them before using.

Serves 4

INGREDIENTS

2 medium-size ripe mangoes

1¼ cups chicken stock

2 large skinless duck breasts, about 8 ounces each

2 garlic cloves, crushed

1 tsp grated fresh ginger root

3 tbsp vegetable oil

1 tsp wine vinegar

1 tsp light soy sauce

1 leek, sliced

chopped fresh parsley, to garnish

---

1 Peel the mangoes and cut the flesh from each side of the pits. Cut the flesh into strips.

2 Put half the mango pieces and the stock in a food processor and process until smooth. Alternatively, press half the mangoes through a fine strainer and mix with the stock.

3 Rub the garlic and ginger over the duck. Heat the oil in a preheated wok and cook the duck breasts, turning, until sealed. Reserve the oil in the wok and remove the duck. Place the duck on a rack set over a roasting pan and cook in a preheated oven, at 425°F for 20 minutes, until completely cooked through.

4 Meanwhile, place the mango and stock mixture in a saucepan and add the vinegar and soy sauce. Bring to a boil and cook over a high heat, stirring, until reduced by half.

5 Heat the oil reserved in the wok. Add the leek and remaining mango and stir-fry for 1 minute. Remove from the wok, transfer to a warm serving dish, and keep warm.

6 Slice the cooked duck breasts and arrange the slices on top of the leek and mango mixture. Pour the sauce over the duck slices, garnish, and serve.

COOK'S TIP

Do not overcook the mango slices in the wok, or stir too vigorously, otherwise they will break up.

Stir-Fried Duck with Broccoli & Bell Peppers

*This is a colorful dish using different colored bell peppers
and broccoli to make it both tasty and appealing to the eye.*

Serves 4

INGREDIENTS

1 egg white
2 tbsp cornstarch
1 pound skinless, boneless duck
vegetable oil, for deep-frying
1 red bell pepper, seeded and diced

1 yellow bell pepper, seeded
  and diced
4^1/$_2$ ounces small broccoli florets
1 garlic clove, crushed
2 tbsp light soy sauce

2 tsp Chinese rice wine or dry sherry
1 tsp light brown sugar
^{1}/$_2$ cup chicken stock
2 tsp sesame seeds

1 Beat the egg white and cornstarch together in a mixing bowl.

2 Cut the duck into 1-inch cubes and stir into the egg white mixture. Let stand for 30 minutes.

3 Heat the oil for deep-frying in a preheated wok until almost smoking. Remove the duck from the egg white mixture, add to the wok, and fry in the oil for 4–5 minutes, until crisp. Remove the duck from the oil with a slotted spoon and drain well on paper towels.

4 Add the bell peppers and broccoli to the wok and stir-fry for 2–3 minutes. Remove with a slotted spoon and drain well on paper towels.

5 Pour all but 2 tablespoons of the oil from the wok and return to the heat. Add the garlic and stir-fry for 30 seconds. Stir in the soy sauce, Chinese rice wine or sherry, sugar, and stock and bring to a boil.

6 Stir in the duck and reserved vegetables and cook for 1–2 minutes.

7 Carefully spoon the duck and vegetables onto a warm serving dish and sprinkle with the sesame seeds. Serve immediately.

Pork Fry with Vegetables

This is a very simple dish that lends itself to almost any combination of vegetables that you have on hand.

Serves 4

INGREDIENTS

12 ounces lean pork tenderloin
2 tbsp vegetable oil
2 garlic cloves, crushed
$^{1}/_{2}$-inch piece fresh ginger root, cut into slivers
1 red bell pepper, seeded and diced

1 carrot, peeled and cut into thin strips
1 fennel bulb, sliced
1 ounce canned water chestnuts, drained and halved
$2\,^{3}/_{4}$ ounces bean sprouts

2 tbsp Chinese rice wine
$1\,^{1}/_{4}$ cups pork or chicken stock
pinch of dark brown sugar
1 tsp cornstarch
2 tsp water

1 Cut the pork into thin slices. Heat the oil in a preheated wok. Add the garlic, ginger, and pork and stir-fry for 1–2 minutes, until the meat is sealed.

2 Add the bell pepper, carrot, fennel, and water chestnuts to the wok and stir-fry for about 2-3 minutes.

3 Add the bean sprouts and stir-fry for 1 minute. Remove the pork and vegetables from the wok and keep warm.

4 Add the Chinese rice wine, pork or chicken stock, and sugar to the wok. Blend the cornstarch to a smooth paste with the water and stir it into the sauce. Bring to a boil, stirring constantly until thickened and clear.

5 Return the meat and vegetables to the wok and cook for 1–2 minutes, until thoroughly heated through and well coated with the sauce. Transfer to a warm serving dish and serve immediately.

COOK'S TIP

Use dry sherry instead of the Chinese rice wine if you have difficulty obtaining it.

Sweet & Sour Pork

This dish is a popular choice in Western diets, and must be one of the best known of Chinese recipes.

Serves 4

INGREDIENTS

vegetable oil, for deep-frying
8 ounces pork tenderloin, cut into
 $1/2$-inch cubes
1 onion, sliced
1 green bell pepper, seeded
 and sliced
8 ounces pineapple pieces
1 small carrot, peeled and cut into
 thin strips

1 ounce canned bamboo shoots,
 drained, rinsed, and halved
rice or noodles, to serve

BATTER:
1 cup all-purpose flour
1 tbsp cornstarch
$1^1/_2$ tsp baking powder
1 tbsp vegetable oil

SAUCE:
$2/_3$ cup light brown sugar
2 tbsp cornstarch
$1/_2$ cup white
 wine vinegar
2 garlic cloves, crushed
4 tbsp tomato paste
6 tbsp pineapple juice

1 To make the batter, sift the flour into a mixing bowl, together with the cornstarch and baking powder. Add the oil and stir in just enough water to make a thick, smooth batter (about $3/_4$ cup).

2 Pour about $2/_3$ cup of the vegetable oil into a wok and heat until almost smoking. Lower the heat slightly. Dip the cubes of pork into the batter, and cook in the hot oil, in batches, for 2–3 minutes or until the pork is cooked through. Remove from the wok with a slotted spoon and keep warm.

3 Drain all but 1 tablespoon of oil from the wok and return it to the heat. Add the onion, bell pepper, pineapple pieces, carrot, and bamboo shoots and stir-fry for 1–2 minutes. Remove from the wok with a slotted spoon and set aside.

4 Mix all the sauce ingredients together until thoroughly combined and pour the mixture into the wok. Bring to a boil, stirring until thickened and clear. Cook for 1 minute, then return the pork and vegetables to the wok. Cook for a further 1–2 minutes and serve with rice or noodles.

Pork with Plums

*Plum sauce is often used in Chinese cooking with duck
or other rich, fatty meat to counteract the flavor.*

Serves 4

INGREDIENTS

1 pound pork tenderloin
1 tbsp cornstarch
2 tbsp light soy sauce
2 tbsp Chinese rice wine
4 tsp light brown sugar
pinch of ground cinnamon

5 tsp vegetable oil
2 garlic cloves, crushed
2 scallions, chopped
4 tbsp plum sauce
1 tbsp hoisin sauce
$^2/_3$ cup water

dash of chili sauce
fried plum quarters and scallions,
   to garnish

1 Cut the pork tenderloin into thin slices.

2 Mix together the cornstarch, soy sauce, Chinese rice wine, sugar, and ground cinnamon.

3 Place the pork in a shallow dish and pour the cornstarch mixture over it. Cover and marinate for at least 30 minutes.

4 Carefully remove the pork from the dish, reserving the marinade.

5 Heat the oil in a preheated wok. Add the pork and stir-fry for 3–4 minutes, until lightly colored golden brown.

6 Stir in the garlic, scallions, plum sauce, hoisin sauce, water, and chili sauce. Bring the sauce to a boil. Reduce the heat, cover, and simmer for 8–10 minutes, or until the pork is cooked through and tender.

7 Stir in the reserved marinade and cook, stirring, for about

5 minutes. Transfer to a warm serving dish and garnish with fried plum quarters and scallions. Serve immediately.

VARIATION

*Strips of boneless duck may be
used instead of the pork,
if desired.*

Deep-fried Pork Fritters

Small pieces of pork are coated in a light batter and deep-fried in this recipe—they are delicious dipped in a soy and honey sauce.

Serves 4

INGREDIENTS

1 pound pork tenderloin
2 tbsp peanut oil
1³/₄ cups all-purpose flour
2 tsp baking powder
1 egg, beaten
1 cup milk

pinch of chili powder
vegetable oil, for deep-frying

SAUCE:
2 tbsp dark soy sauce
3 tbsp clear honey

1 tbsp wine vinegar
1 tbsp chopped chives
1 tbsp tomato paste
chives, to garnish

---

1 Cut the pork tenderloin into 1-inch cubes.

2 Heat the peanut oil in a preheated wok. Add the pork and stir-fry for 2-3 minutes, until sealed. Remove the pork with a slotted spoon and set aside until it is required.

3 Sift the flour and baking powder into a bowl and make a well in the center. Gradually beat in the egg, milk, and chili powder to make a thick batter.

4 Heat the oil for deep-frying in a wok until almost smoking, then reduce the heat slightly.

5 Toss the pork pieces in the batter to coat thoroughly. Add the pork to the wok and deep-fry for 2–3 minutes or until golden brown and cooked through. Remove with a slotted spoon and drain on absorbent paper towels.

6 Meanwhile, mix together the soy sauce, honey, wine vinegar, chives, and tomato paste and spoon the dipping sauce into a small serving bowl.

7 Transfer the pork fritters to serving dishes, garnish with chives, and serve with the sauce.

COOK'S TIP

Be careful when heating the oil for deep-frying. It must be heated so that it is almost smoking, then the heat must be reduced immediately. Place the pork in the oil carefully.

Beef & Broccoli Stir-fry

This is a great combination of ingredients in terms of color and flavor,
and it is so simple and quick to prepare.

Serves 4

INGREDIENTS

8 ounces lean steak, trimmed
2 garlic cloves, crushed
dash of chili oil
1/2-inch piece fresh ginger
   root, grated

1/2 tsp Chinese five-spice powder
2 tbsp dark soy sauce
2 tbsp vegetable oil
5 ounces broccoli florets
1 tbsp light soy sauce

2/3 cup beef stock
2 tsp cornstarch
4 tsp water
carrot strips, to garnish

1 Cut the steak into thin strips and place in a shallow glass dish. Mix together the garlic, chili oil, grated ginger, Chinese five-spice powder, and soy sauce in a small bowl and pour the mixture over the beef, tossing to coat the strips evenly. Marinate in the refrigerator for 30 minutes.

2 Heat 1 tablespoon of the oil in a preheated wok. Add the broccoli and stir-fry over a medium heat for 4–5 minutes. Remove from the wok with a slotted spoon and set aside.

3 Heat the remaining vegetable oil in the wok. Add the steak strips, together with the marinade, and stir-fry for about 2-3 minutes, until the steak is browned all over and sealed.

4 Return the broccoli to the wok and stir in the soy sauce and stock.

5 Blend the cornstarch with the water to form a smooth paste and stir it into the wok. Bring to a boil, stirring until thickened and clear. Cook for 1 minute.

6 Transfer the beef and broccoli stir-fry to a warm serving dish, arrange the carrot strips in a lattice pattern on top, and serve immediately.

COOK'S TIP

Marinate the steak for several hours for a fuller flavor. Cover and marinate in the refrigerator if preparing in advance.

Marinated Beef With Oyster Sauce

*This dish is quick to cook, but benefits from lengthy marinating,
as this tenderizes and flavors the meat.*

Serves 4

INGREDIENTS

8 ounces lean steak, cut into
   1-inch cubes
1 tbsp light soy sauce
1 tsp sesame oil
2 tsp Chinese rice wine or
   dry sherry
1 tsp superfine sugar
2 tsp hoisin sauce
1 garlic clove, crushed
$^1/_2$ tsp cornstarch

2 tbsp vegetable oil
3 garlic cloves, crushed
$^1/_2$-inch piece fresh ginger
   root, grated
8 baby corncobs, halved lengthwise
$^1/_2$ green bell pepper, seeded and
   thinly sliced
1 ounce canned bamboo shoots,
   drained and rinsed

green bell pepper slices,
   to garnish
rice or noodles, to serve

SAUCE:
2 tbsp dark soy sauce
1 tsp superfine sugar
$^1/_2$ tsp cornstarch
3 tbsp oyster sauce
8 tbsp water

1 Place the steak in a shallow dish. Mix together the soy sauce, sesame oil, Chinese rice wine or sherry, sugar, hoisin sauce, garlic, and cornstarch and pour the mixture over the steak, turning it to coat. Cover and marinate for at least 1 hour.

2 Meanwhile, make the sauce. Mix the dark soy sauce with the sugar, cornstarch, oyster sauce, and water. Heat the oil in a preheated wok. Add the steak, together with the marinade, and stir-fry for 2–3 minutes, until sealed and lightly browned.

3 Add the garlic, ginger, baby corn cobs, bell pepper, and bamboo shoots. Stir in the oyster sauce mixture and bring to a boil.

Reduce the heat and cook for 2–3 minutes. Transfer to a warm serving dish, garnish with green bell pepper slices, and serve immediately with rice or noodles.

COOK'S TIP

For a fuller flavor, marinate the beef in the refrigerator overnight.

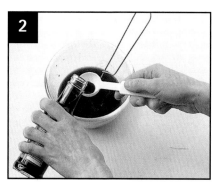

Spicy Beef

In this recipe beef is marinated in a five-spice
and chili marinade for a spicy flavor.

Serves 4

INGREDIENTS

8 ounces fillet steak
2 garlic cloves, crushed
1 tsp powdered star anise
1 tbsp dark soy sauce
scallion tassels, to garnish (optional)

SAUCE:
2 tbsp vegetable oil
1 bunch scallions, halved lengthwise
1 tbsp dark soy sauce

1 tbsp dry sherry
1/4 tsp chili sauce
2/3 cup water
2 tsp cornstarch
4 tsp water

1 Cut the steak into thin strips and place in a shallow dish.

2 Mix together the garlic, star anise, and dark soy sauce in a bowl and pour the mixture over the steak strips, turning them to ensure that they are thoroughly coated. Cover with plastic wrap and marinate in the refrigerator for at least 1 hour, preferably overnight.

3 Heat the oil in a preheated wok. Reduce the heat slightly, add the halved scallions and stir-fry for 1-2 minutes. Remove from the wok with a slotted spoon and set aside.

4 Add the beef to the wok, together with the marinade, and stir-fry for 3–4 minutes. Return the halved scallions to the wok and add the soy sauce, sherry, chili sauce and the water.

5 Blend the cornstarch to a paste with the 4 tsp water and stir into the wok. Bring to a boil, stirring until the sauce thickens and clears.

6 Transfer to a warm serving dish, garnish with scallion tassels, if using, and serve immediately.

COOK'S TIP

Omit the chili sauce for a
milder dish.

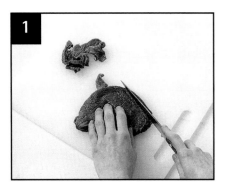

Beef & Beans

*The green of the beans complements the dark color
of the beef, served in a rich sauce.*

Serves 4

INGREDIENTS

1 pound fillet steak, cut into
  1-inch pieces

MARINADE:
2 tsp cornstarch
2 tbsp dark soy sauce
2 tsp peanut oil

SAUCE:
2 tbsp vegetable oil
3 garlic cloves, crushed
1 small onion, cut into 8 sections
8 ounces thin green beans, halved
$^1/_4$ cup unsalted cashews
1 ounce canned bamboo shoots,
  drained and rinsed

2 tsp dark soy sauce
2 tsp Chinese rice wine or dry sherry
$^1/_2$ cup beef stock
2 tsp cornstarch
4 tsp water
salt and pepper

1 To make the marinade,
mix together the cornstarch,
soy sauce and peanut oil.

2 Place the steak in a shallow
glass bowl. Pour the
marinade over the steak, turn to
coat thoroughly, cover, and
marinate in the refrigerator for at
least 30 minutes.

3 To make the sauce, heat the
oil in a preheated wok. Lower
the heat slightly, add the garlic,

onion, beans, cashews, and
bamboo shoots, and stir-fry for
2–3 minutes.

4 Remove the steak from the
marinade, drain, add to the
wok, and stir-fry for 3–4 minutes.

5 Mix the soy sauce, Chinese
rice wine or sherry, and beef
stock together. Blend the
cornstarch with the water to make
a smooth paste and add to the soy
sauce mixture, mixing to combine.

6 Stir the mixture into the wok
and bring the sauce to a boil,
stirring until thickened and clear.
Reduce the heat and simmer for
2–3 minutes. Season to taste and
serve immediately.

VARIATION

*This recipe would also be
delicious with the addition of sugar
snap peas instead of the beans,
if desired.*

Lamb Meatballs

These small meatballs are made with ground lamb and flavored with chili, garlic, parsley, and Chinese curry powder.

Serves 4

INGREDIENTS

1 pound ground lamb
3 garlic cloves, crushed
2 scallions, finely chopped
$^{1}/_{2}$ tsp chili powder
1 tsp Chinese curry powder

1 tbsp chopped fresh parsley
$^{1}/_{2}$ cup fresh white breadcrumbs
1 egg, beaten
3 tbsp vegetable oil
$4^{1}/_{2}$ ounces Chinese
   cabbage, shredded
1 leek, sliced

1 tbsp cornstarch
2 tbsp water
$1^{1}/_{4}$ cups lamb stock
1 tbsp dark soy sauce
shredded leek, to garnish

1 Mix the lamb, garlic, scallions, chili powder, Chinese curry powder, parsley, and breadcrumbs together in a bowl. Work the egg into the mixture, bringing it together to form a firm mixture. Roll into 16 small, even-size balls.

2 Heat the oil in a preheated wok. Add the cabbage and leek and stir-fry for 1 minute. Remove from the wok with a slotted spoon and set aside.

3 Add the meatballs to the wok and fry in batches, turning gently, for 3-4 minutes, until golden brown all over.

4 Mix the cornstarch and water together to form a smooth paste and set aside. Pour the lamb stock and soy sauce into the wok and cook for 2–3 minutes. Stir in the cornstarch paste. Bring to a boil and cook, stirring constantly, until the sauce has thickened and become clear.

5 Return the cabbage and leek to the wok and cook for 1 minute, until heated through. Arrange the cabbage and leek on a warm serving dish, top with the meatballs, garnish with shredded leek, and serve immediately.

VARIATION

Use ground pork or beef instead of the lamb as an alternative.

Lamb with Mushroom Sauce

*Use a lean cut of lamb, such as fillet, for this recipe
for both flavor and tenderness.*

Serves 4

INGREDIENTS

12 ounces lean boneless lamb, such
  as fillet or loin
2 tbsp vegetable oil
3 garlic cloves, crushed
1 leek, sliced
1 tsp cornstarch

4 tbsp light soy sauce
3 tbsp Chinese rice wine or
  dry sherry
3 tbsp water
$^{1}/_{2}$ tsp chili sauce
6 ounces large mushrooms, sliced

$^{1}/_{2}$ tsp sesame oil
fresh red chili strips, to garnish

1 Using a sharp knife, cut the lamb into thin strips.

2 Heat the oil in a preheated wok. Add the lamb strips, garlic, and leek and stir-fry for about 2-3 minutes.

3 Mix together the cornstarch, soy sauce, Chinese rice wine or dry sherry, water, and chili sauce in a bowl until thoroughly combined and set aside.

4 Add the mushrooms to the wok and stir-fry for 1 minute.

5 Stir in the sauce and cook for 2–3 minutes, or until the lamb is cooked through and tender. Sprinkle the sesame oil over the top and transfer to a warm serving dish. Garnish with red chili strips and serve immediately.

COOK'S TIP

*Use rehydrated dried Chinese
mushrooms obtainable from
specialty shops or Chinese
grocery stores for a really
authentic flavor.*

VARIATION

*The lamb can be replaced
with lean steak or pork
tenderloin in this classic recipe
from Beijing. You could also
use 2–3 scallions, 1 shallot,
or 1 small onion instead of
the leek, if desired.*

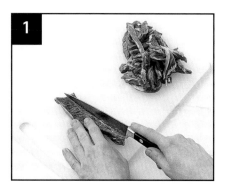

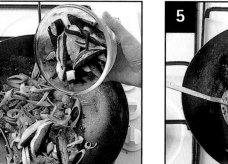

Lamb with Garlic Sauce

This dish contains Szechuan pepper which is quite hot
and may be replaced with black pepper, if desired.

Serves 4

INGREDIENTS

1 pound lamb fillet or loin
2 tbsp dark soy sauce
2 tsp sesame oil
2 tbsp Chinese rice wine or dry sherry
$\frac{1}{2}$ tsp Szechuan pepper

4 tbsp vegetable oil
4 garlic cloves, crushed
2 ounces canned water chestnuts,
 drained and quartered

1 green bell pepper, seeded
 and sliced
1 tbsp wine vinegar
1 tbsp sesame oil

1 Cut the lamb into 1-inch pieces and place them in a shallow dish.

2 Mix together 1 tablespoon of the soy sauce, the sesame oil, Chinese rice wine or sherry, and Szechuan pepper. Pour the mixture over the lamb, turning to coat, and marinate for at least 30 minutes.

3 Heat the vegetable oil in a preheated wok. Remove the lamb from the marinade and add to the wok, together with the garlic. Stir-fry for 2–3 minutes.

4 Add the water chestnuts and bell pepper to the wok and stir-fry for 1 minute.

5 Add the remaining soy sauce and the wine vinegar, mixing together well.

6 Add the sesame oil and cook, stirring constantly, for 1–2 minutes, or until the lamb is heated through.

7 Transfer the lamb and garlic sauce to a warm serving dish and serve immediately.

COOK'S TIP

Sesame oil is used as a flavoring, rather than for frying, as it burns readily, hence it is added at the end of cooking.

VARIATION

Chinese chives, also known as garlic chives, would make an appropriate garnish for this dish.

Hot Lamb

This is quite a spicy dish, using two chilies in the rich sauce. Halve the number of chilies to reduce the heat or seed the chilies before using, if desired.

Serves 4

INGREDIENTS

1 pound lean, boneless lamb
2 tbsp hoisin sauce
1 tbsp dark soy sauce
1 garlic clove, crushed
2 tsp grated fresh ginger root
2 tbsp vegetable oil
2 onions, sliced

1 fennel bulb, sliced
4 tbsp water

SAUCE:
1 large fresh red chili, cut into
   thin strips

1 fresh green chili, cut into
   thin strips
2 tbsp rice wine vinegar
2 tsp light brown sugar
2 tbsp peanut oil
1 tsp sesame oil

1 Cut the lamb into 1-inch cubes and place in a shallow glass dish.

2 Mix together the hoisin sauce, soy sauce, garlic, and ginger in a bowl and pour over the lamb, turning to coat well. Marinate in the refrigerator for 20 minutes.

3 Heat the vegetable oil in a preheated wok. Add the lamb and stir-fry for 1–2 minutes.

4 Add the onions and fennel to the wok and cook for a further 2 minutes, or until they are just beginning to brown.

5 Stir in the water, cover, and cook for 2–3 minutes.

6 To make the sauce, place the chilies, rice wine vinegar, sugar, peanut oil, and sesame oil in a saucepan and cook over a low heat for 3-4 minutes, stirring to combine.

7 Transfer the lamb and onions to a warm serving dish, pour the sauce on top, toss lightly, and serve immediately.

VARIATION

Use beef, pork, or duck instead of the lamb and vary the vegetables, using leeks or celery instead of the onion and fennel.

Sesame Lamb Stir-Fry

This is a very simple but delicious dish, in which lean pieces of lamb are cooked in sugar and soy sauce and sprinkled with sesame seeds, then served on a bed of leeks and carrot.

Serves 4

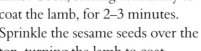

INGREDIENTS

1 pound boneless lean lamb

2 tbsp peanut oil

1 carrot, peeled and cut into
  matchsticks

2 leeks, sliced

2 garlic cloves, crushed

$1/3$ cup lamb or vegetable stock

2 tsp light brown sugar

1 tbsp dark soy sauce

$4^1/2$ tsp sesame seeds

1 Cut the lamb into thin strips. Heat the peanut oil in a preheated wok. Add the lamb and stir-fry for 2–3 minutes. Remove the lamb from the wok with a slotted spoon and set aside.

2 Add the carrot, leek, and garlic to the wok and stir-fry in the remaining oil for 1–2 minutes. Remove from the wok with a slotted spoon and set aside. Drain any remaining oil from the wok.

3 Place the stock, sugar, and soy sauce in the wok and add the lamb. Cook, stirring constantly to coat the lamb, for 2–3 minutes. Sprinkle the sesame seeds over the top, turning the lamb to coat.

4 Spoon the leek mixture onto a warm serving dish and top with the lamb. Serve immediately.

VARIATION

This recipe would be equally delicious made with strips of skinless chicken or turkey breast or with shrimp. The cooking times remain the same.

COOK'S TIP

Be careful not to burn the sugar in the wok when heating and coating the meat, otherwise the flavor of the dish will be spoiled.

Vegetables

Vegetables play a very important role in the Chinese diet and are used extensively in all meals. It is perfectly possible to enjoy a meal from a selection of the following recipes contained in this chapter, without including meat or fish.

The Chinese enjoy their vegetables crisp, so cooking times in this chapter reflect this factor in order to bring out the flavors and textures of the ingredients used, as well as preserving the vitamins and the brightness of the colors. There are main course dishes and a variety of side dishes, all of which bring out the full potential of vegetables.

When selecting vegetables for cooking, the Chinese attach great importance to the freshness of the ingredients used. Always buy crisp, firm vegetables, and cook them as soon as possible. Another point to remember is to wash the vegetables just before cutting, in order to avoid losing vitamins in water, and to cook them as soon as they have been cut so that the vitamin content is not lost through evaporation.

Spicy Eggplants

*Try to obtain the smaller Chinese eggplants for this dish, as they have
a slightly sweeter taste, but the recipe is just as delicious with the larger variety.*

Serves 4

INGREDIENTS

1 pound eggplants, rinsed
2 tsp salt
3 tbsp vegetable oil
2 garlic cloves, crushed

1-inch piece fresh ginger
  root, chopped
1 onion, halved and sliced
1 fresh red chili, sliced
2 tbsp dark soy sauce
1 tbsp hoisin sauce

$^1/_2$ tsp chili sauce
1 tbsp dark brown sugar
1 tbsp wine vinegar
1 tsp ground Szechuan pepper
$1^1/_4$ cups vegetable stock

1 Cut the eggplants into cubes if you are using the larger variety, or cut the smaller type in half. Place the eggplants in a colander and sprinkle with the salt. Set aside for 30 minutes to let the bitter juices drain. Rinse the eggplants under cold running water and pat dry with absorbent paper towels.

2 Heat the oil in a preheated wok and add the garlic, ginger, onion, and fresh chili. Stir-fry for 30 seconds and add the eggplants. Continue to cook for 1–2 minutes.

3 Add the soy sauce, hoisin sauce, chili sauce, sugar, wine vinegar, Szechuan pepper, and vegetable stock to the wok, reduce the heat, and simmer, uncovered, for about 10 minutes, or until the eggplants are cooked through and tender. Increase the heat and boil to reduce the sauce until thickened enough to coat the eggplants. Serve the spicy eggplants immediately.

COOK'S TIP

Sprinkling the eggplants with salt and letting them stand removes the bitter juices, which would otherwise taint the flavor of the dish.

Fried Bean Curd & Vegetables

Bean curd may be obtained from both Chinese and Western supermarkets.
It is available in different forms, the cake form being used in this recipe.

Serves 4

INGREDIENTS

1 pound bean curd
$^2/_3$ cup vegetable oil
1 leek, sliced
4 baby corncobs, halved lengthwise
2 ounces snow peas
1 red bell pepper, seeded and diced

2 ounces canned bamboo shoots,
    drained and rinsed
rice or noodles, to serve

SAUCE:
1 tbsp Chinese rice wine or
    dry sherry

4 tbsp oyster sauce
3 tsp light soy sauce
2 tsp superfine sugar
pinch of salt
$^1/_4$ cup vegetable stock
1 tsp cornstarch
2 tsp water

1 Rinse the bean curd in cold water and pat thoroughlydry with absorbent paper towels. Cut the bean curd into 1-inch cubes.

2 Heat the oil in a preheated wok until almost smoking. Reduce the heat, add the bean curd, and gently stir-fry until golden brown. Remove from the wok with a slotted spoon and drain thoroughly on absorbent paper towels.

3 Pour all but 2 tablespoons of the oil from the wok and return to the heat. Add the leek, corncobs, snow peas, bell pepper, and bamboo shoots and stir-fry for 2–3 minutes.

4 Add the Chinese rice wine or sherry, oyster sauce, soy sauce, sugar, salt, and vegetable stock to the wok and bring to a boil. Blend the cornstarch with the water to form a smooth paste and stir it into the sauce. Bring the sauce to a boil

and cook, stirring constantly, until thickened and clear.

5 Stir the bean curd into the mixture in the wok and cook for about 1 minute until completely heated through. Serve with rice or noodles.

COOK'S TIP

Use marinated or smoked bean curd for extra flavor.

Bean Curd Casserole

Bean curd is the perfect ingredient for absorbing all the other flavors contained in this dish.
If marinated bean curd is used, it will add a flavor of its own.

Serves 4

INGREDIENTS

1 pound bean curd
2 tbsp peanut oil
8 scallions, cut
   into sticks
2 celery stalks, sliced
4¹/₂ ounces broccoli florets

4¹/₂ ounces zucchini, sliced
2 garlic cloves, thinly sliced
1 pound fresh baby spinach
rice, to serve

SAUCE:
2 cups vegetable stock
2 tbsp light soy sauce
3 tbsp hoisin sauce
¹/₂ tsp chili powder
1 tbsp sesame oil

1 Cut the bean curd into 1-inch cubes and set aside.

2 Heat the oil in a preheated wok. Add the scallions, celery, broccoli, zucchini, garlic, spinach, and bean curd and stir-fry for 3–4 minutes.

3 To make the sauce, mix together the vegetable stock, soy sauce, hoisin sauce, chili powder, and sesame oil in a flameproof casserole and bring to a boil. Add the vegetables and bean curd, reduce the heat, cover, and simmer for 10 minutes. Transfer to a warm serving dish and serve immediately with rice.

COOK'S TIP

This recipe has a green vegetable theme, but alter the color and flavor by adding your favorite vegetables.

VARIATION

Add 3 ounces fresh or canned and drained straw mushrooms with the vegetables in step 2.

Marinated Bean Sprouts & Vegetables

This dish is served cold as a salad or appetizer and is very easy to make. It is a form of cold chop suey.

Serves 4

INGREDIENTS

1 pound bean sprouts
2 fresh red chilies
1 red bell pepper, seeded and
   thinly sliced

1 green bell pepper, seeded and
   thinly sliced
2 ounces canned water chestnuts,
   drained and quartered
1 celery stalk, sliced

3 tbsp rice wine vinegar
2 tbsp light soy sauce
2 tbsp chopped chives
1 garlic clove, crushed
pinch of Chinese curry powder

1 Place the bean sprouts, chilies, bell peppers, water chestnuts, and celery in a large bowl and mix together well.

2 Mix together the rice wine vinegar, soy sauce, chives, garlic, and Chinese curry powder in a bowl and pour the mixture over the prepared vegetables. Toss to mix thoroughly.

3 Cover the salad and chill for at least 3 hours. Drain the vegetables thoroughly, transfer to a serving dish, and serve.

COOK'S TIP

There are hundreds of varieties of chilies and it is not always possible to tell how hot they are going to be. As a general rule, dark green chilies are hotter than light green and red chilies. Thin, pointed chilies are usually hotter than fatter, blunter chilies. However, there are always exceptions and even chilies from the same plant can vary considerably in their degree of spiciness.

COOK'S TIP

This dish is delicious with Chinese roasted meats or served with the marinade and noodles.

Honey-fried Chinese Cabbage

*This vegetable is similar to lettuce in that the leaves
are delicate with a sweet flavor.*

Serves 4

INGREDIENTS

1 pound Chinese cabbage
1 tbsp peanut oil
$^1/_2$-inch piece fresh ginger root,
　grated
2 garlic cloves, crushed

1 fresh red chili, sliced
1 tbsp Chinese rice wine or dry sherry
$4^1/_2$ tsp light soy sauce
1 tbsp clear honey

$^1/_2$ cup orange juice
1 tbsp sesame oil
2 tsp sesame seeds
orange zest, to garnish

1 Separate the Chinese cabbage leaves and shred them finely, using a sharp knife.

2 Heat the peanut oil in a preheated wok. Add the ginger, garlic, and chili to the wok and stir-fry the mixture for about 30 seconds.

3 Add the shredded Chinese cabbage, Chinese rice wine or sherry, soy sauce, honey, and orange juice to the wok. Reduce the heat slightly and simmer for 5 minutes.

4 Add the sesame oil, sprinkle the sesame seeds on top, and mix to combine. Transfer to a warm serving dish, garnish with the orange zest, and serve immediately.

COOK'S TIP

Single-flower honey has a better, more individual flavor than blended honey. Acacia honey is typically Chinese, but you could also try clover, lemon blossom, lime flower, or orange blossom.

VARIATION

Use a western cabbage, such as Savoy, instead of Chinese cabbage if they are unavailable. The flavor will be slightly different and the color darker, but it will still taste just as delicious.

Green Stir-fry

The basis of this recipe is bok choy, sometimes known as pak choi or Chinese greens.
If unavailable, use Swiss chard or Savoy cabbage instead.

Serves 4

INGREDIENTS

2 tbsp peanut oil
2 garlic cloves, crushed
1/2 tsp ground star anise
1 tsp salt

12 ounces bok choy, shredded
8 ounces fresh baby spinach
1 ounce snow peas
1 celery stalk, sliced

1 green bell pepper, seeded
  and sliced
1/4 cup vegetable stock
1 tsp sesame oil

1 Heat the peanut oil in a preheated wok.

2 Lower the heat slightly. Add the crushed garlic to the wok and stir-fry for about 30 seconds. Stir in the star anise, salt, bok choy, spinach, snow peas, celery, and green bell pepper and stir-fry for 3–4 minutes.

3 Add the stock, cover, and cook for 3–4 minutes.

4 Remove the lid from the wok and stir in the sesame oil. Mix thoroughly.

5 Transfer the stir-fry to a warm serving dish and serve.

COOK'S TIP

Star anise is an important ingredient in Chinese cuisine. The attractive star-shaped pods are often used whole to add a decorative garnish to dishes. The flavor is similar to licorice but with spicy undertones, and is quite strong. Together with cassia, cloves, fennel seeds, and Szechuan pepper, dried star anise is used to make Chinese five-spice powder.

COOK'S TIP

Serve this dish as part of a vegetarian meal or alternatively, with roast meats.

Crisp Fried Cabbage & Almonds

This dish is better known as crispy seaweed. It does not actually contain seaweed, but consists of collard greens or bok choy, deep-fried and sprinkled with salt and cinnamon.

Serves 4

INGREDIENTS

2 pounds bok choy or collard greens
3 cups vegetable oil
3/4 cup blanched almonds

1 tsp salt
1 tbsp light brown sugar
pinch of ground cinnamon

1 Separate the leaves from the bok choy or collard greens and rinse them well. Pat thoroughly dry with paper towels.

2 Shred the greens into thin strips, using a sharp knife.

3 Heat the vegetable oil in a preheated wok until it is almost smoking.

4 Reduce the heat and add the greens. Cook for about 2–3 minutes, or until the greens begin to float in the oil and have become crisp.

5 Remove the greens from the oil with a slotted spoon and drain thoroughly on absorbent paper towels.

6 Add the almonds to the oil in the wok and cook for 30 seconds. Carefully remove the almonds from the oil with a slotted spoon.

7 Mix the salt, sugar, and cinnamon together and sprinkle onto the greens. Toss the almonds into the greens. Transfer to a warm serving dish and serve the "seaweed" immediately.

COOK'S TIP

Ensure that the greens are completely dry before adding them to the oil, otherwise it will spit. The greens will not become crisp if they are wet when placed in the oil.

Creamy Green Vegetables

This dish is very quick to make. The Chinese cabbage complements the leek perfectly.
A dash of cream is added to the sauce, but this may be omitted if desired.

Serves 4

INGREDIENTS

1 pound Chinese cabbage, shredded	1¹/₄ cups vegetable stock	2 tbsp light cream or unsweetened
2 tbsp peanut oil	1 tbsp light soy sauce	yogurt
2 leeks, shredded	2 tsp cornstarch	1 tbsp chopped cilantro
4 garlic cloves, crushed	4 tsp water	

1 Blanch the Chinese cabbage in boiling water for 30 seconds. Drain, plunge into cold water or rinse under cold running water, then drain thoroughly again.

2 Heat the oil in a preheated wok and add the Chinese cabbage, leeks, and garlic. Stir-fry for 2–3 minutes.

3 Add the vegetable stock and soy sauce to the wok, reduce the heat to low, cover, and simmer for 10 minutes, or until the vegetables are tender.

4 Remove the vegetables from the wok with a slotted spoon and set aside. Bring the stock to a boil and boil vigorously until reduced by about half.

5 Blend the cornstarch with the water to form a smooth paste and stir the mixture into the stock. Bring to a boil, and cook, stirring constantly, until the stock has thickened and become clear.

6 Reduce the heat and stir in the vegetables and cream or yogurt. Cook over a low heat for 1 minute.

7 Transfer to a serving dish, sprinkle with the chopped cilantro, and serve.

COOK'S TIP

Do not boil the sauce once the cream or yogurt has been added, as it will separate.

Stir-Fried Cucumber with Chilies

Warm cucumbers are absolutely delicious, especially when combined with the heat of chili and the flavor of ginger.

Serves 4

INGREDIENTS

2 medium cucumbers
2 tsp salt
1 tbsp vegetable oil
2 garlic cloves, crushed

$^{1}/_{2}$-inch fresh ginger root, grated
2 fresh red chilies, chopped
2 scallions, chopped
1 tsp yellow bean sauce

1 tbsp clear honey
$^{1}/_{2}$ cup water
1 tsp sesame oil

1 Peel the cucumbers and cut in half lengthwise. Scrape the seeds from the center with a teaspoon and discard.

2 Cut the cucumber into strips and place on a plate. Sprinkle the salt over the cucumber strips and set aside for about 20–25 minutes. Rinse well under cold running water and pat dry with absorbent paper towels.

3 Heat the oil in a preheated wok until it is almost smoking. Lower the heat slightly and add the garlic, ginger, chilies, and scallions and stir-fry for 30 seconds.

4 Add the cucumbers to the wok, together with the yellow bean sauce and honey. Stir-fry for a further 30 seconds.

5 Add the water and cook over a high heat until most of the water has evaporated.

6 Sprinkle the sesame oil over the cucumber and chili stir-fry. Transfer to a warm serving dish and serve immediately.

COOK'S TIP

The cucumber is sprinkled with salt and let stand in order to draw out the excess water, thus preventing a soggy meal!

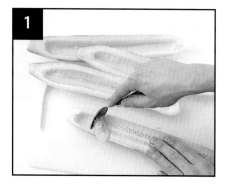

Spicy Mushrooms

A mixture of mushrooms common in Western cooking has been used in this recipe for a richly flavored dish. If Chinese dried mushrooms are available, add a small quantity for texture.

Serves 4

INGREDIENTS

2 tbsp peanut oil
2 garlic cloves, crushed
3 scallions, chopped
10 ounces button mushrooms
2 large open-cap mushrooms, sliced

4$^{1}/_{2}$ ounces oyster mushrooms
1 tsp chili sauce
1 tbsp dark soy sauce
1 tbsp hoisin sauce
1 tbsp wine vinegar

$^{1}/_{2}$ tsp ground Szechuan pepper
1 tbsp dark brown sugar
1 tsp sesame oil
chopped fresh parsley, to garnish

1 Heat the oil in a preheated wok until almost smoking. Reduce the heat slightly, add the garlic and scallions, and stir-fry for 30 seconds.

2 Add the mushrooms, chili sauce, soy sauce, hoisin sauce, vinegar, pepper, and sugar and stir-fry for 4–5 minutes, or until the mushrooms are cooked.

3 Sprinkle the sesame oil on top. Transfer to a warm serving dish, garnish with parsley, and serve immediately.

COOK'S TIP

Chinese mushrooms are used more for their unusual texture than for their flavor. Tree ears are widely used and are available dried from Chinese grocery stores. They should be rinsed, soaked in warm water for about 20 minutes, and rinsed again before use. Straw mushrooms, so called because they grow on straw, are available, fresh or canned, from Chinese grocery stores and some supermarkets. They have a slippery texture.

COOK'S TIP

This dish is ideal served with rich meat or fish dishes.

Garlic Spinach

This has to be one of the simplest recipes, yet it is so tasty. Spinach is quickly fried with garlic and lemon grass and tossed in a little soy sauce and sugar.

Serves 4

INGREDIENTS

2 pounds fresh spinach
2 tbsp peanut oil
2 garlic cloves, crushed

1 tsp chopped lemon grass
pinch of salt

1 tbsp dark soy sauce
2 tsp brown sugar

1 Carefully remove the coarse stems from the spinach. Rinse the spinach leaves in cold water and drain them thoroughly, patting them dry with absorbent paper towels.

2 Heat the oil in a preheated wok until it is almost smoking.

3 Reduce the heat slightly, add the garlic and lemon grass, and stir-fry for 30 seconds.

4 Add the spinach and salt to the wok and stir-fry for 2–3 minutes, or until the spinach has wilted.

5 Stir in the dark soy sauce and brown sugar and cook for a further 3–4 minutes. Transfer to a warm serving dish and serve immediately.

COOK'S TIP

Lemon grass is widely used in Asian cooking. It is available fresh, dried, canned, or bottled. Dried lemon grass must be soaked for 2 hours before using. The stems are hard and are usually used whole and removed from the dish before serving. The roots can be crushed or finely chopped.

COOK'S TIP

Use baby spinach, if possible, as the leaves have a better flavor and look more appealing. If using baby spinach, the stems may be left intact.

Chinese Fried Vegetables

The Chinese are known for their colorful, crisp vegetables, quickly stir-fried. This recipe demonstrates how tasty they are, tossing them in a soy and hoisin sauce.

Serves 4

INGREDIENTS

2 tbsp peanut oil
12 ounces broccoli florets
1 tbsp chopped fresh ginger root
2 onions, cut into 8 sections
3 celery stalks, sliced
6 ounces fresh baby spinach

$4^1/2$ ounces snow peas
6 scallions, quartered
2 garlic cloves, crushed

SAUCE:
2 tbsp light soy sauce
2 tsp superfine sugar
2 tbsp dry sherry
1 tbsp hoisin sauce
$2/3$ cup vegetable stock

1 Heat the peanut oil in a preheated wok until it is almost smoking.

2 Add the broccoli florets, ginger, onions, and celery and stir-fry for 1 minute.

3 Add the spinach, snow peas, scallions, and garlic and stir-fry for 3–4 minutes.

4 Mix together the soy sauce, sugar, sherry, hoisin sauce, and stock and pour into the wok, mixing well to coat the vegetables. Cover and cook over a medium heat for 2–3 minutes, or until the vegetables are cooked through, but still crisp. Transfer to a warm serving dish and serve immediately.

COOK'S TIP

You could use this mixture to fill Chinese pancakes. They are available from Chinese grocery stores and can be reheated in a steamer in 2–3 minutes.

VARIATION

Any vegetables may be used in this recipe, depending on your preference and its seasonal availability.

Vegetable Chop Suey

Make sure that the vegetables are all cut into pieces of a similar size in this recipe, so that they cook within the same amount of time.

Serves 4

INGREDIENTS

1 yellow bell pepper, seeded
1 red bell pepper, seeded
1 carrot, peeled
1 zucchini
1 fennel bulb
1 onion

2 ounces snow peas
2 tbsp peanut oil
3 garlic cloves, crushed
1 tsp grated fresh ginger root
$4^{1}/_{2}$ ounces bean sprouts
2 tsp light brown sugar

2 tbsp light soy sauce
$^{1}/_{2}$ cup vegetable stock

1 Cut the yellow and red bell peppers, carrot, zucchini, and fennel into very thin slices. Cut the onion into quarters and then cut each quarter in half. Slice the snow peas diagonally to create the maximum surface area.

2 Heat the oil in a preheated wok until it is almost smoking. Lower the heat slightly, add the garlic and ginger, and stir-fry for 30 seconds. Add the onion and stir-fry for a further 30 seconds.

3 Add the bell peppers, carrot, zucchini, fennel, and snow peas to the wok and stir-fry for 2 minutes.

4 Add the bean sprouts to the wok and stir in the sugar, soy sauce, and stock. Reduce the heat to low and simmer for about 1–2 minutes, until the vegetables are tender and coated in the sauce.

5 Transfer the vegetables and sauce to a serving dish and serve immediately.

COOK'S TIP

Use any combination of colorful vegetables that you have on hand to make this versatile dish.

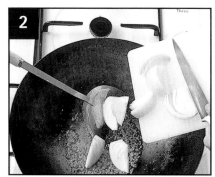
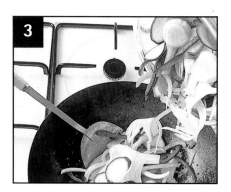

Vegetable Sesame Stir-fry

Sesame seeds add a delicious flavor to any recipe and are particularly good with vegetables in this soy and rice wine or sherry sauce.

Serves 4

INGREDIENTS

2 tbsp vegetable oil	2 ounces button mushrooms	$^1/_2$ tsp Chinese curry powder
3 garlic cloves, crushed	1 leek, sliced	2 tbsp light soy sauce
1 tbsp sesame seeds, plus extra to garnish	1 zucchini, sliced	1 tbsp Chinese rice wine or dry sherry
2 celery stalks, sliced	1 small red bell pepper, seeded and sliced	1 tsp sesame oil
2 baby corncobs, sliced	1 fresh green chili, sliced	1 tsp cornstarch
	2 ounces Chinese cabbage, shredded	4 tbsp water

1 Heat the oil in a preheated wok until it is almost smoking. Lower the heat slightly, add the garlic and sesame seeds, and stir-fry for 30 seconds.

2 Add the celery, baby corn, mushrooms, leek, zucchini, bell pepper, chili, and Chinese cabbage and stir-fry for 4–5 minutes, until the vegetables are beginning to soften.

3 Mix together the Chinese curry powder, soy sauce, Chinese rice wine or sherry, sesame oil, cornstarch, and water and stir the mixture into the wok. Bring to a boil and cook, stirring constantly, until the sauce thickens and clears. Cook for 1 minute, spoon into a warm serving dish, sprinkle sesame seeds on top, and serve immediately.

VARIATION

You could substitute oyster sauce for the soy sauce, if desired.

COOK'S TIP

The ingredients are fried in vegetable oil in this recipe and not peanut oil, as this would overpower the wonderful flavor of the sesame seeds. However, peanut oil could be used if desired.

Green Bean Stir-fry

*These beans are simply cooked in a spicy, hot sauce
for a tasty and very easy recipe.*

Serves 4

INGREDIENTS

1 pound thin green beans
2 fresh red chilies
2 tbsp peanut oil

1/2 tsp ground star anise
1 garlic clove, crushed
2 tbsp light soy sauce

2 tsp clear honey
1/2 tsp sesame oil

1 Using a sharp knife, cut the green beans in half.

2 Slice the fresh chilies, seeding them first if you prefer a milder dish.

3 Heat the oil in a preheated wok until almost smoking.

4 Lower the heat slightly, add the green beans, and stir-fry for 1 minute.

5 Add the sliced red chilies, star anise, and garlic to the wok and stir-fry for a further 30 seconds.

6 Mix together the soy sauce, honey, and sesame oil and stir into the wok. Cook for 2 minutes, tossing the beans in the sauce to coat. Transfer the beans to a warm serving dish and serve immediately.

VARIATION

*This recipe is surprisingly delicious
made with Brussels sprouts instead
of green beans. Trim the sprouts,
then shred them finely. Stir-fry
the sprouts in hot oil for 2 minutes,
then proceed with the recipe
from step 4.*

COOK'S TIP

*This dish makes a great
accompaniment to fish or lightly
cooked meats with a mild flavor.*

Vegetable Rolls

In this recipe a mixed vegetable stuffing is wrapped in Chinese cabbage and steamed until tender. Serve with chili or soy sauce for a really tasty meal.

Serves 4

INGREDIENTS

8 large Chinese cabbage leaves

FILLING:
2 baby corncobs, sliced
1 carrot, peeled and finely chopped
1 celery stalk, chopped

4 scallions, chopped
1 ounce canned water chestnuts, drained and chopped
2 tbsp unsalted cashews, chopped
1 garlic clove, chopped
1 tsp grated fresh ginger root

1 ounce canned bamboo shoots, drained, rinsed, and chopped
1 tsp sesame oil
2 tsp soy sauce

1 Place the Chinese cabbage leaves in a large bowl and pour boiling water over them to soften them. Set aside for 1 minute and drain thoroughly.

2 Mix together the baby corncobs, carrot, celery, scallions, water chestnuts, cashews, garlic, ginger, and bamboo shoots in a bowl.

3 Mix together the sesame oil and soy sauce and add to the vegetables, mixing thoroughly.

4 Spread out the Chinese cabbage leaves on a board and spoon an equal quantity of the filling mixture onto each leaf.

5 Roll the leaves up, folding in the sides, to make neat packets. Secure the packets with one or two toothpicks.

6 Place the filled rolls in a small heatproof dish in a steamer, cover, and cook for 15–20 minutes, until the packets are cooked. Serve with a sauce of your choice.

COOK'S TIP

Make the packets in advance, cover, and store in the refrigerator until required, then steam according to the recipe.

Eight Jewel Vegetables

This recipe, as the title suggests, is a colorful mixture of eight vegetables,
cooked in a black bean and soy sauce.

Serves 4

INGREDIENTS

2 tbsp peanut oil
6 scallions, sliced
3 garlic cloves, crushed
1 green bell pepper, seeded
  and diced
1 red bell pepper, seeded and diced

1 fresh red chili, sliced
2 tbsp chopped water chestnuts
1 zucchini, chopped
4^1/$_2$ ounces oyster mushrooms
3 tbsp black bean sauce
2 tsp Chinese rice wine or dry sherry

4 tbsp dark soy sauce
1 tsp dark brown sugar
2 tbsp water
1 tsp sesame oil

1 Heat the peanut oil in a preheated wok until it is almost smoking.

2 Lower the heat slightly, add the sliced scallions and the garlic, and stir-fry for about 30 seconds.

3 Add the bell peppers, chili, water chestnuts, and zucchini to the wok and stir-fry for 2–3 minutes, or until the vegetables are just beginning to soften.

4 Add the mushrooms, black bean sauce, Chinese rice wine or sherry, soy sauce, sugar, and water to the wok and stir-fry for a further 4 minutes.

5 Sprinkle with sesame oil and serve immediately.

VARIATION

Add 8 ounces diced, marinated bean curd to this recipe for a main course for 4 people.

COOK'S TIP

Eight jewels or treasures form a traditional part of the Chinese New Year celebrations, which start in the last week of the old year. The Kitchen God, an important figure, is sent to give a report to heaven, returning on New Year's Eve in time for the feasting.

Spicy Vegetarian Fried Triangles

Marinated bean curd is ideal in this recipe for added flavor,
although the spicy coating is very tasty with plain bean curd.

Serves 4

INGREDIENTS

1 tbsp sea salt
4¹/₂ tsp Chinese five-spice powder
3 tbsp light brown sugar

2 garlic cloves, crushed
1 tsp grated fresh ginger root
2 x 8 ounce cakes bean curd

vegetable oil, for deep-frying
2 leeks, shredded and halved
shredded leek, to garnish

1 Mix the salt, Chinese five-spice powder, sugar, garlic, and ginger in a bowl and transfer to a plate.

2 Cut the bean curd cakes in half diagonally to form two triangles. Cut each triangle in half, and then in half again to form 16 triangles.

3 Roll the bean curd triangles in the spice mixture, turning to coat thoroughly. Set aside for 1 hour.

4 Heat the oil for deep-frying in a wok until it is almost smoking. Reduce the heat slightly, add the bean curd triangles, and fry for 5 minutes, until golden brown. Remove from the wok with a slotted spoon, set aside, and keep warm.

5 Add the leeks to the wok and stir-fry for 1 minute. Remove from the wok with a slotted spoon and drain on absorbent paper towels.

6 Arrange the leeks on a warm serving plate and place the fried bean curd on top. Garnish with the fresh shredded leek and serve immediately.

COOK'S TIP

Fry the bean curd in batches and keep each batch warm until all the bean curd has been fried and is ready to serve.

Chinese Vegetable Casserole

*This mixed vegetable casserole is very versatile and is delicious
with any combination of vegetables of your choice.*

Serves 4

INGREDIENTS

4 tbsp vegetable oil
2 medium carrots, peeled and sliced
1 zucchini, sliced
4 baby corncobs, halved lengthwise
4^1/$_2$ ounces cauliflower florets
1 leek, sliced

4^1/$_2$ ounces canned water chestnuts,
  drained and halved
8 ounces bean curd, diced
1^1/$_4$ cups vegetable stock
1 tsp salt
2 tsp dark brown sugar

2 tsp dark soy sauce
2 tbsp dry sherry
1 tbsp cornstarch
2 tbsp water
1 tbsp chopped cilantro,
  to garnish

1 Heat the vegetable oil in a
preheated wok until it is
almost smoking.

2 Lower the heat slightly, add
the carrots, zucchini,
corncobs, cauliflower florets, and
leek to the wok and stir-fry for
2–3 minutes.

3 Stir in the water chestnuts,
bean curd, stock, salt, sugar,
soy sauce, and sherry and bring to
a boil. Reduce the heat, cover, and
simmer for 20 minutes.

4 Blend the cornstarch with
the water, mixing to form a
smooth paste.

5 Remove the lid from the
wok and stir in the cornstarch
mixture. Bring the sauce to a boil
and cook, stirring constantly, until
it has thickened slightly and
become clear.

6 Transfer the casserole to a
warm serving dish, sprinkle
with chopped cilantro, and serve
immediately.

COOK'S TIP

*If there is too much liquid
remaining, boil vigorously for
1 minute before adding the
cornstarch to reduce
it slightly.*

Bamboo Shoots, Ginger, & Bell Peppers

This dish has a wonderfully strong ginger flavor, which is integral to Chinese cooking. The mixed bell peppers give the otherwise insipid bamboo shoots a burst of color.

Serves 4

INGREDIENTS

2 tbsp peanut oil

8 ounces canned bamboo shoots, drained and rinsed

1-inch piece fresh ginger root, finely chopped

1 small red bell pepper, seeded and thinly sliced

1 small green bell pepper, seeded and thinly sliced

1 small yellow bell pepper, seeded and thinly sliced

1 leek, sliced

$^1/_2$ cup vegetable stock

1 tbsp light soy sauce

2 tsp light brown sugar

2 tsp Chinese rice wine or dry sherry

1 tsp cornstarch

2 tsp water

1 tsp sesame oil

1 Heat the peanut oil in a preheated wok.

2 Add the bamboo shoots, ginger, bell peppers, and leek to the wok and stir-fry for 2–3 minutes.

3 Stir in the stock, soy sauce, sugar, and Chinese rice wine or sherry and bring to a boil, stirring. Reduce the heat and simmer for 4–5 minutes, or until the vegetables begin to soften.

4 Blend the cornstarch with the water to form a smooth paste.

5 Stir the cornstarch paste into the wok. Bring to a boil and cook, stirring constantly, until the sauce has thickened and become clear.

6 Sprinkle the sesame oil over the vegetables and cook for 1 minute. Transfer to a warm serving dish and serve immediately.

COOK'S TIP

Add a chopped fresh red chili or a few drops of chili sauce for a spicier dish.

Bamboo Shoots with Spinach

In this recipe, spinach is fried with spices and then braised in a soy-flavored sauce with bamboo shoots for a rich, delicious dish.

Serves 4

INGREDIENTS

3 tbsp peanut oil
8 ounces fresh spinach, chopped
6 ounces canned bamboo shoots,
    drained and rinsed
1 garlic clove, crushed

2 fresh red chilies, sliced
pinch of ground cinnamon
1¼ cups vegetable stock
pinch of sugar

pinch of salt
1 tbsp light soy sauce

1 Heat the peanut oil in a preheated wok.

2 Add the spinach and bamboo shoots to the wok and stir-fry for 1 minute.

3 Add the garlic, chili, and cinnamon to the mixture in the wok and stir-fry for a further 30 seconds.

4 Stir in the vegetable stock, sugar, salt, and soy sauce, cover, and cook over a medium heat for 5 minutes, or until the vegetables are cooked through and the sauce has reduced. Transfer the bamboo shoots and spinach to a warm serving dish and serve.

COOK'S TIP

Fresh bamboo shoots are rarely available in the West and, in any case, are extremely time-consuming to prepare. Canned bamboo shoots are quite satisfactory, as they are used to provide a crunchy texture, rather than for their flavor.

COOK'S TIP

If there is too much liquid after 5 minutes cooking in step 4, blend a little cornstarch with double the quantity of cold water and stir into the sauce.

Sweet & Sour Bean Curd with Vegetables

Sweet-and-sour sauce was one of the first Chinese sauces introduced to Western diets, and remains one of the most popular. It is ideal with meat, fish, or vegetables, as in this recipe.

Serves 4

INGREDIENTS

2 celery stalks
1 carrot, peeled
1 green bell pepper
3 ounces snow peas
2 tbsp vegetable oil
2 garlic cloves, crushed

8 baby corncobs
4^1/$_2$ ounces bean sprouts
1 pound bean curd, cubed
rice or noodles, to serve

SAUCE:
2 tbsp light brown sugar
2 tbsp wine vinegar
1 cup vegetable stock
1 tsp tomato paste
1 tbsp cornstarch

1 Thinly slice the celery and cut the carrot into thin strips. Seed and dice the bell pepper and cut the snow peas in half diagonally.

2 Heat the vegetable oil in a preheated wok until it is almost smoking. Reduce the heat slightly, add the garlic, celery, carrot, bell pepper, snow peas, and corncobs, and stir-fry for about 3–4 minutes.

3 Add the bean sprouts and bean curd to the wok and cook for 2 minutes, stirring well.

4 Combine the brown sugar, wine vinegar, vegetable stock, tomato paste, and cornstarch, stirring well to mix. Stir into the wok, bring to a boil, and cook, stirring constantly, until the sauce thickens and clears. Continue to cook for 1 minute. Serve with rice or noodles.

COOK'S TIP

Be careful not to break up the bean curd when stirring.

Gingered Broccoli

*Ginger and broccoli is a perfect combination of flavors
and make an exceptionally tasty side dish.*

Serves 4

INGREDIENTS

2 tbsp peanut oil

1 garlic clove, crushed

2-inch piece fresh ginger root,
   finely chopped

1^1/$_2$ pounds broccoli florets

1 leek, sliced

2^3/$_4$ ounces canned water chestnuts,
   drained and halved

^{1}/$_2$ tsp superfine sugar

^{1}/$_2$ cup vegetable stock

1 tsp dark soy sauce

1 tsp cornstarch

2 tsp water

1 Heat the oil in a preheated wok. Add the garlic and ginger and stir-fry for 30 seconds. Add the broccoli, leek, and water chestnuts and stir-fry for a further 3–4 minutes.

2 Add the sugar, stock, and soy sauce, reduce the heat, and simmer for 4–5 minutes, or until the broccoli is almost cooked.

3 Blend the cornstarch with the water to form a smooth paste and stir it into the wok. Bring to a boil and cook, stirring constantly, for 1 minute, until thickened. Transfer to a warm serving dish and serve immediately.

VARIATION

You could substitute water spinach for the broccoli. Trim the woody ends and cut the remainder into 2-inch lengths, keeping the stalks and leaves separate. Add the stalks with the leek in step 1 and add the leafy parts 2 minutes later. Reduce the cooking time in step 2 to 3–4 minutes.

COOK'S TIP

If you prefer a slightly milder ginger flavor, cut the ginger into larger strips, stir-fry as described, and then remove from the wok and discard.

Chinese Potato Sticks

These potato sticks are a variation of the great Western favorite, being flavored with soy sauce and chili.

Serves 4

INGREDIENTS

1¹/₂ pounds medium-size potatoes
8 tbsp vegetable oil
1 fresh red chili, halved
1 small onion, quartered

2 garlic cloves, halved
2 tbsp soy sauce
pinch of salt

1 tsp wine vinegar
1 tbsp coarse sea salt
pinch of chili powder

1 Peel the potatoes and cut into thin slices along their length. Cut the slices into matchsticks.

2 Blanch the potato sticks in boiling water for 2 minutes, drain, rinse under cold water, and drain well again. Pat thoroughly dry with absorbent paper towels.

3 Heat the oil in a preheated wok until it is almost smoking. Add the chili, onion, and garlic and stir-fry for 30 seconds. Remove and discard the chili, onion and garlic.

4 Add the potato sticks to the oil and fry for 3–4 minutes, or until golden.

5 Add the soy sauce, salt, and vinegar to the wok, reduce the heat, and fry for 1 minute, or until the potatoes are crisp.

6 Remove the potatoes with a slotted spoon and drain on absorbent paper towels.

7 Transfer the potato sticks to a serving dish, sprinkle with the sea salt and chili powder, and serve immediately.

VARIATION

Sprinkle other flavorings over the cooked potato sticks, such as curry powder, or serve with a chili dip.

Cucumber & Bean Sprout Salad

This is a very light dish and is ideal on its own
for a summer meal or as a starter.

Serves 4

INGREDIENTS

12 ounces bean sprouts
1 small cucumber
1 green bell pepper, seeded and cut
   into matchsticks
1 carrot, peeled and cut into
   matchsticks

2 tomatoes, finely chopped
1 celery stalk, cut into matchsticks

DRESSING:
1 garlic clove, crushed
dash of chili sauce

2 tbsp light soy sauce
1 tsp wine vinegar
2 tsp sesame oil
16 fresh chives

1 Blanch the bean sprouts in boiling water for 1 minute. Drain well and rinse under cold water. Drain thoroughly again.

2 Cut the cucumber in half lengthwise. Scoop out the seeds with a teaspoon and discard. Cut the flesh into matchsticks and mix with the bean sprouts, green bell pepper, carrot, tomatoes, and celery.

3 Mix together the garlic, chili sauce, soy sauce, vinegar, and sesame oil. Pour the dressing over the vegetables, tossing well to coat. Spoon onto 4 individual serving plates. Garnish with fresh chives and serve.

VARIATION

You could substitute 12 ounces cooked, cooled green beans or snow peas for the cucumber. Vary the bean sprouts for a different flavor. Try adzuki bean or alfalfa sprouts, as well as the better-known mung and soy bean sprouts.

COOK'S TIP

The vegetables may be prepared in advance, but do not assemble the dish until just before serving, otherwise the bean sprouts will discolor.

Rice & Noodles

No Chinese cookbook would be complete without
recipes for rice and noodle dishes. Many
people believe that they should always serve rice
with a savory meal, and although it is often an
excellent choice, there are many wonderful noodle
dishes that can be served in its place.

Nevertheless, this chapter includes some delicious rice
recipes that may be served as accompaniments
or on their own. The Chinese use long-grain, short-
grain, or glutinous rice, and real experts would never
use "minute" rice. Use whatever you are able to obtain
for the recipes that follow and enjoy them! Fried rice is
the most popular rice in Western restaurants, and so
several variations have been included in this chapter.

A wide variety of noodles are available, made from
wheat, buckwheat, or rice flours. Noodles are used to
their full potential in this chapter to bring you delicious
accompaniments and main courses.

Egg Fried Rice

This is a classic Chinese rice dish that has become very popular in the Western diet. Boiled rice is fried with peas, scallions, and egg and flavored with soy sauce.

Serves 4

INGREDIENTS

²/₃ cup long-grain rice
3 eggs, beaten
2 tbsp vegetable oil
2 garlic cloves, crushed

4 scallions, chopped
1 cup cooked peas
1 tbsp light soy sauce

salt
shredded scallion, to garnish

1 Cook the rice in a saucepan of lightly salted boiling water for 10-12 minutes, until almost cooked, but not soft. Drain well, rinse under cold water, and drain thoroughly again.

2 Place the beaten eggs in a saucepan and cook over a gentle heat, stirring lightly until softly scrambled.

3 Heat the oil in a preheated wok. Reduce the heat slightly, add the garlic, scallions, and peas, and sauté, stirring occasionally, for 1-2 minutes.

4 Stir the rice into the wok, mixing to combine.

5 Add the eggs, soy sauce, and salt to taste and stir to mix the egg in thoroughly.

6 Transfer to a warm serving dish and serve garnished with the shredded scallion.

VARIATION

You may choose to add shrimp, ham, or chicken, or a combination in step 3.

COOK'S TIP

The rice is rinsed under cold water to wash out the starch and prevent it from sticking together.

Fried Rice with Pork

*This dish is a meal in itself, containing pieces of pork,
fried with rice, peas, tomatoes, and mushrooms.*

Serves 4

INGREDIENTS

$^2/_3$ cup long-grain rice

3 tbsp peanut oil

1 large onion, cut into 8 sections

8 ounces pork tenderloin,
  thinly sliced

2 open-cap mushrooms, sliced

2 garlic cloves, crushed

1 tbsp light soy sauce

1 tsp light brown sugar

2 tomatoes, peeled, seeded,
  and chopped

$^1/_2$ cup cooked peas

2 eggs, beaten

salt

1 Cook the rice in a saucepan of lightly salted boiling water for about 15 minutes, until tender, but not soft. Drain well, rinse under cold running water, and drain again thoroughly.

2 Heat the oil in a preheated wok. Add the onion and pork and stir-fry for 3-4 minutes, until just beginning to color.

3 Add the mushrooms and garlic to the wok and stir-fry for 1 minute.

4 Add the soy sauce and sugar to the mixture in the wok and stir-fry for a further 2 minutes.

5 Stir in the rice, tomatoes, and peas, mixing well. Transfer the mixture to a warm dish.

6 Stir the eggs into the wok and cook, stirring, for 2-3 minutes, until beginning to set.

7 Return the rice mixture to the wok and mix well. Transfer to a warm serving dish and serve immediately.

COOK'S TIP

You can cook the rice in advance and chill or freeze it until required.

Vegetable Fried Rice

This dish can be served as part of a substantial meal for a number of people or as a vegetarian meal in itself for four.

Serves 4

INGREDIENTS

²/₃ cup long-grain white rice
3 tbsp peanut oil
2 garlic cloves, crushed
¹/₂ tsp Chinese five-spice powder
¹/₃ cup green beans

1 green bell pepper, seeded
 and chopped
4 baby corncobs, sliced
1 ounce canned bamboo shoots,
 drained, rinsed, and chopped

3 tomatoes, peeled, seeded,
 and chopped
¹/₂ cup cooked peas
1 tsp sesame oil
salt

---

1 Cook the rice in a saucepan of lightly salted boiling water for about 15 minutes. Drain well, rinse under cold running water, and drain thoroughly again.

2 Heat the peanut oil in a preheated wok.

3 Add the garlic and Chinese five-spice powder and stir-fry for 30 seconds.

4 Add the green beans, bell pepper, and corncobs and stir-fry for 2 minutes.

5 Stir the bamboo shoots, tomatoes, peas, and rice into the mixture in the wok and stir-fry for 1 further minute.

6 Sprinkle the vegetable fried rice with sesame oil and transfer to a warm serving dish. Serve immediately.

VARIATION

You could add cashews, dry-fried until lightly browned, in step 5 if desired.

COOK'S TIP

Use a selection of vegetables of your choice in this recipe, cutting them to a similar size in order to ensure that they cook in the same amount of time.

Green-fried Rice

Spinach is used in this recipe to give the rice a wonderful green coloring.
Tossed with the carrot strips, it is a really appealing dish.

Serves 4

INGREDIENTS

²/₃ cup long-grain rice	1 tsp grated fresh ginger root	8 ounces fresh baby spinach
2 tbsp vegetable oil	1 carrot, peeled and cut	2 tsp light soy sauce
2 garlic cloves, crushed	into matchsticks	2 tsp light brown sugar
	1 zucchini, diced	salt

1 Cook the rice in a large saucepan of lightly salted boiling water for about 15 minutes. Drain the rice well, rinse under cold running water, and then rinse thoroughly again.

2 Heat the vegetable oil in a preheated wok.

3 Reduce the heat slightly, add the garlic and ginger to the wok, and stir-fry for about 30 seconds.

4 Add the carrot and zucchini to the wok and stir-fry for about 2 minutes.

5 Add the baby spinach and stir-fry for 1 minute, until wilted.

6 Add the rice, soy sauce, and sugar to the wok and mix together well.

7 Transfer the green-fried rice to a warm serving dish and serve immediately.

COOK'S TIP

Light soy sauce has more flavor than the sweeter, dark soy sauce, which gives the food a rich, reddish color.

VARIATION

Chinese cabbage may be used instead of the spinach, giving a lighter green color to the dish.

Special Fried Rice

This dish is a popular choice in Chinese restaurants. Ham and shrimp are mixed with vegetables in a soy-flavored rice.

Serves 4

INGREDIENTS

$^2/_3$ cup long-grain rice
2 tbsp vegetable oil
2 eggs, beaten
2 garlic cloves, crushed

1 tsp grated fresh ginger root
3 scallions, sliced
$^3/_4$ cup cooked peas
$^2/_3$ cup bean sprouts

$1^1/_3$ cups shredded ham
$5^1/_2$ ounces peeled, cooked shrimp
2 tbsp light soy sauce
salt

1 Cook the rice in a saucepan of lightly salted boiling water for about 15 minutes. Drain well, rinse under cold water, and drain thoroughly again.

2 Heat 1 tablespoon of the oil in a preheated wok and add the beaten eggs and a further 1 teaspoon of oil. Tilt the wok so that the egg covers the base to make a thin pancake. Cook until lightly browned on the underside, then flip the pancake over and cook on the other side for about 1 minute. Remove from the wok and cool.

3 Heat the remaining oil in the wok. Add the garlic and ginger and stir-fry for 30 seconds.

4 Add the scallions, peas, bean sprouts, ham, and shrimp to the wok and stir-fry for about 2 minutes.

5 Stir in the soy sauce and rice and cook for a further 2 minutes. Transfer the rice to a serving dish.

6 Roll up the pancake, slice it very thinly and use to garnish the rice. Serve immediately.

COOK'S TIP

As this recipe contains meat and fish, it is ideal served with simpler vegetable dishes.

Chicken & Rice Casserole

This is a spicy casserole of rice, chicken, vegetables, and chili in a soy- and ginger-flavored sauce. Although called a casserole, the dish requires only 30 minutes cooking time.

Serves 4

INGREDIENTS

$^2/_3$ cup long-grain rice
2 tsp salt
1 tbsp dry sherry
2 tbsp light soy sauce
2 tbsp dark soy sauce
2 tsp dark brown sugar
1 tsp sesame oil

2 pounds skinless, boneless chicken, diced
3$^3/_4$ cups chicken stock
2 open-cap mushrooms, sliced
2 ounces canned water chestnuts, drained and halved
3 ounces broccoli florets

1 yellow bell pepper, seeded and sliced
4 tsp grated fresh ginger root
whole chives, to garnish

1 Cook the rice in a saucepan of boiling water with half the salt for about 15 minutes. Drain well, rinse under cold water, and drain again thoroughly.

2 Place the sherry, soy sauce, sugar, remaining salt, and sesame oil in a large bowl and mix together until well combined.

3 Stir the chicken into the soy mixture, turning to coat well. Marinate in the refrigerator for about 30 minutes.

4 Bring the stock to a boil in a preheated wok.

5 Add the chicken with the marinade, mushrooms, water chestnuts, broccoli, bell pepper, and ginger.

6 Stir in the rice, reduce the heat, cover, and cook for 25–30 minutes, until the chicken and vegetables are cooked through.

7 Transfer to a serving dish, garnish with chives, and serve.

VARIATION

This dish would work equally well with beef or pork. Chinese dried mushrooms may be used instead of the open-cap mushrooms, if rehydrated before adding to the dish.

Crab Fried Rice

Canned crab meat is used in this recipe for convenience, but fresh white crab meat could be used—quite deliciously—in its place.

Serves 4

INGREDIENTS

²/₃ cup long-grain rice
2 tbsp peanut oil
4¹/₂ ounces canned white crab
   meat, drained

1 leek, sliced
²/₃ cup bean sprouts
2 eggs, beaten
1 tbsp light soy sauce

2 tsp lime juice
1 tsp sesame oil
sliced lime, to garnish

1 Cook the rice in a saucepan of boiling salted water for 15 minutes. Drain well, rinse under cold running water, and drain again thoroughly.

2 Heat the peanut oil in a preheated wok.

3 Add the crab meat, leek, and bean sprouts to the wok and stir-fry for 2-3 minutes. Remove the mixture with a slotted spoon and set aside until required.

4 Add the eggs to the wok and cook, stirring occasionally, for 2-3 minutes, until they are just beginning to set.

5 Stir the rice and the crab meat, leek, and bean sprout mixture into the eggs in the wok.

6 Add the soy sauce and lime juice to the mixture in the wok. Cook for 1 minute, stirring to combine, and sprinkle with the sesame oil.

7 Transfer the crab fried rice to a warm serving dish, garnish with the sliced lime, and serve immediately.

VARIATION

Cooked lobster may be used instead of the crab for a really special dish.

Fried Vegetable Noodles

In this recipe, noodles are first boiled and then deep-fried for
a crisply textured dish, and tossed with fried vegetables.

Serves 4

INGREDIENTS

3 cups dried egg noodles

2 tbsp peanut oil

2 garlic cloves, crushed

$^1/_2$ tsp ground star anise

1 carrot, peeled and cut into
matchsticks

1 green bell pepper, seeded and cut
into matchsticks

1 onion, quartered and sliced

$4^1/_2$ ounces broccoli florets

3 ounces bamboo shoots

1 celery stalk, sliced

1 tbsp light soy sauce

$^2/_3$ cup vegetable stock

oil, for deep-frying

1 tsp cornstarch

2 tsp water

1 Cook the noodles in boiling water for 1-2 minutes. Drain well and rinse under cold running water. Leave to drain in a colander.

2 Heat the oil in a preheated wok until smoking. Reduce the heat, add the garlic and star anise, and stir-fry for 30 seconds. Add the remaining vegetables and stir-fry for 1-2 minutes.

3 Add the soy sauce and stock to the wok and cook over a low heat for 5 minutes.

4 Heat the oil for deep-frying until a cube of bread browns in 30 seconds.

5 Form the drained noodles into rounds and deep-fry them in batches until crisp, turning once. Drain thoroughly on paper towels.

6 Blend the cornstarch with the water to form a smooth paste and stir into the wok. Bring to a boil, stirring until the sauce is thickened and clear.

7 Arrange the noodles on a warm serving plate, spoon the vegetables on top, and serve immediately.

COOK'S TIP

 Make sure that the noodles are very dry before adding them to the hot oil, otherwise the oil will spit.

Chicken Noodles

Rice noodles are used in this recipe. They are available in large supermarkets or Chinese grocery stores. If unavailable, egg noodles may be used in their place.

Serves 4

INGREDIENTS

8 ounces rice noodles

2 tbsp peanut oil

8 ounces skinless, boneless chicken breast, sliced

2 garlic cloves, crushed

1 tsp grated fresh ginger root

1 tsp Chinese curry powder

1 red bell pepper, seeded and thinly sliced

3 ounces snow peas, shredded

1 tbsp light soy sauce

2 tsp Chinese rice wine

2 tbsp chicken stock

1 tsp sesame oil

1 tbsp chopped fresh cilantro

1 Soak the rice noodles for 4 minutes in warm water. Drain thoroughly and set aside until required.

2 Heat the oil in a preheated wok. Add the chicken, and stir-fry for 2–3 minutes.

3 Add the garlic, ginger, and curry powder and stir-fry for a further 30 seconds.

4 Add the bell pepper and snow peas; stir-fry for 2-3 minutes.

5 Add the drained noodles, the soy sauce, Chinese rice wine, and chicken stock to the wok and mix well, stirring occasionally, for 1 minute.

6 Sprinkle the sesame oil and chopped cilantro over the noodles and vegetables.

7 Transfer the noodles and vegetables to a warm serving dish and serve immediately.

VARIATION

You can use pork or duck in this recipe instead of the chicken, if desired.

Curried Shrimp Noodles

These noodles have a fairly strong flavor and are almost a meal in themselves. If served as an accompaniment, they are ideal with plain vegetable or fish dishes.

Serves 4

INGREDIENTS

8 ounces rice noodles
4 tbsp vegetable oil
1 onion, sliced
2 ham slices, shredded
2 tbsp Chinese curry powder

$^2/_3$ cup fish stock
8 ounces peeled, raw shrimp
2 garlic cloves, crushed
6 scallions, chopped

1 tbsp light soy sauce
2 tbsp hoisin sauce
1 tbsp dry sherry
2 tsp lime juice
fresh chives, to garnish

1 Cook the rice noodles in a saucepan of boiling water for 3-4 minutes. Drain well, rinse under cold water, and drain thoroughly again. Set aside until required.

2 Heat 2 tablespoons of the oil in a preheated wok.

3 Add the onion and ham and stir-fry for 1 minute.

4 Add the curry powder to the wok and stir-fry for a further 30 seconds.

5 Stir the noodles and stock into the wok and cook for 2-3 minutes. Remove the noodles from the wok and keep warm.

6 Heat the remaining oil in the wok. Add the shrimp, garlic, and scallions and stir-fry for about 1 minute.

7 Add the soy sauce, hoisin sauce, sherry, and lime juice and stir to combine. Pour the mixture over the noodles, toss to mix, and garnish with fresh chives before serving.

VARIATION

You can use cooked shrimp if you prefer, but toss them into the mixture at the last minute—long enough for them to heat right through. Overcooking will result in tough, inedible shrimp.

Singapore Noodles

This is a special and well-known dish, which is a delicious meal in itself. Packed with chicken, shrimp, and vegetables, it is full of wonderful flavors.

Serves 4

INGREDIENTS

8 ounces dried egg noodles
6 tbsp vegetable oil
4 eggs, beaten
3 garlic cloves, crushed
1 1/2 tsp chili powder

8 ounces skinless, boneless chicken, cut into thin strips
3 celery stalks, sliced
1 green bell pepper, seeded and sliced
4 scallions, sliced

1 ounce canned water chestnuts, drained and quartered
2 fresh red chilies, sliced
10 ounces peeled, cooked shrimp
6 ounces bean sprouts
2 tsp sesame oil

1 Soak the noodles in boiling water for 4 minutes, or until soft. Drain well on absorbent paper towels.

2 Heat 2 tablespoons of the oil in a preheated wok. Add the eggs and stir until set. Remove the cooked eggs from the wok, set aside, and keep warm.

3 Add the remaining oil to the wok. Add the garlic and chili powder and stir-fry for 30 seconds.

4 Add the chicken and stir-fry for 4-5 minutes, until just beginning to turn golden brown on all sides.

5 Stir in the celery, bell pepper, scallions, water chestnuts, and chilies and cook for a further 8 minutes, or until the chicken is cooked through.

6 Add the shrimp and the reserved noodles to the wok, together with the bean sprouts, and toss to mix well.

7 Break the cooked egg with a fork and sprinkle it over the noodles, together with the sesame oil. Serve immediately.

COOK'S TIP

When mixing precooked ingredients into the dish, such as the egg and noodles, ensure that they are heated right through and are hot when ready to serve.

Spicy Pork & Noodles

This is quite a spicy dish, with a delicious peanut flavor.
Increase or reduce the amount of chili to your liking.

Serves 4

INGREDIENTS

12 ounces ground pork
1 tbsp light soy sauce
1 tbsp dry sherry
12 ounces egg noodles
2 tsp sesame oil
2 tbsp vegetable oil

2 garlic cloves, crushed
2 tsp grated fresh ginger root
2 fresh red chilies, sliced
1 red bell pepper, seeded and
　finely sliced

$\frac{1}{4}$ cup unsalted peanuts
3 tbsp peanut butter
3 tbsp dark soy sauce
dash of chili oil
$1\frac{1}{4}$ cups pork stock

1 Mix together the pork, light soy sauce, and dry sherry in a large bowl. Cover and marinate for 30 minutes.

2 Meanwhile, cook the noodles in a saucepan of boiling water for 4 minutes. Drain well, rinse in cold water, and drain again.

3 Toss the noodles in the sesame oil.

4 Heat the vegetable oil in a preheated wok. Add the garlic, ginger, chilies, and red bell pepper and stir-fry for 30 seconds.

5 Add the pork to the mixture in the wok, together with the marinade. Continue cooking for about 1 minute, until the pork is sealed.

6 Add the peanuts, peanut butter, soy sauce, chili oil, and stock and cook for 2-3 minutes.

7 Toss the noodles in the mixture and serve at once.

VARIATION

Ground chicken or lamb would also be excellent in this recipe instead of the pork.

Chicken on Crispy Noodles

Blanched noodles are fried in the wok until crisp and brown, and then topped with a shredded chicken sauce for a delightfully tasty dish.

Serves 4

INGREDIENTS

8 ounces skinless, boneless chicken
  breasts, shredded
1 egg white
5 tsp cornstarch
8 ounces thin egg noodles

$1^2/_3$ cups vegetable oil
$2^1/_2$ cups chicken stock
2 tbsp dry sherry
2 tbsp oyster sauce
1 tbsp light soy sauce

1 tbsp hoisin sauce
1 red bell pepper, seeded and very
  thinly sliced
2 tbsp water
3 scallions, chopped

1 Mix the chicken, egg white, and 2 teaspoons of the cornstarch in a bowl. Let stand for at least 30 minutes.

2 Blanch the noodles in boiling water for 2 minutes, then drain thoroughly. Heat the oil in a preheated wok. Add the noodles, spreading them to cover the base of the wok. Cook over a low heat for about 5 minutes, until the noodles are browned on the underside. Flip the noodles over and brown on the other side.

Remove from the wok when crisp and browned, place on a serving plate, and keep warm. Drain the oil from the wok.

3 Add $1^1/_4$ cups of the chicken stock to the wok. Remove from the heat and add the chicken, stirring well so that it does not stick. Return to the heat and cook for 2 minutes. Drain, discarding the stock.

4 Wipe the wok with paper towels and return to the heat.

Add the sherry, oyster sauce, soy sauce, hoisin sauce, red bell pepper, and the remaining chicken stock and bring to a boil. Blend the remaining cornstarch with the water to form a paste and stir it into the mixture.

5 Return the chicken to the wok and cook over a low heat for 2 minutes. Place the chicken on top of the noodles and sprinkle with scallions. Serve immediately.

Cellophane Noodles with Yellow Bean Sauce

Cellophane or thread noodles are excellent reheated, unlike other noodles which must be served as soon as they are ready.

Serves 4

INGREDIENTS

6 ounces cellophane noodles
1 tbsp peanut oil
1 leek, sliced
2 garlic cloves, crushed

1 pound ground chicken
1 cup chicken stock
1 tsp chili sauce
2 tbsp yellow bean sauce

4 tbsp light soy sauce
1 tsp sesame oil
chopped chives, to garnish

1 Soak the noodles in boiling water for 15 minutes. Drain the noodles thoroughly and cut them into short lengths with a pair of kitchen scissors. Set aside until they are required.

2 Heat the oil in a preheated wok. Add the leek and garlic and stir-fry for 30 seconds.

3 Add the chicken to the wok and stir-fry for 4-5 minutes, until the chicken is completely cooked through.

4 Add the chicken stock, chili sauce, yellow bean sauce, and soy sauce to the wok and cook for 3-4 minutes.

5 Add the drained noodles and sesame oil to the wok and cook, tossing to mix well, for 4-5 minutes.

6 Spoon the cellophane noodles and yellow bean sauce into a warm serving bowl, sprinkle with chopped chives to garnish, and serve immediately.

COOK'S TIP

Cellophane noodles are available from many supermarkets and all Chinese grocery stores.

Noodles with Shrimp

This is a simple dish using egg noodles and large shrimp,
which give the dish a wonderful flavor, texture, and color.

Serves 4

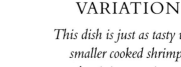

INGREDIENTS

8 ounces thin egg noodles
2 tbsp peanut oil
1 garlic clove, crushed
1/2 tsp ground star anise

1 bunch scallions, cut into
 2-inch pieces
24 raw jumbo shrimp, peeled with
 tails intact

2 tbsp light soy sauce
2 tsp lime juice
lime wedges, to garnish

1 Blanch the noodles in a saucepan of boiling water for about 2 minutes. Drain well, rinse under cold water, and drain thoroughly again.

2 Heat the oil in a preheated wok until almost smoking.

3 Reduce the heat slightly, add the garlic and star anise to the wok, and stir-fry for about 30 seconds.

4 Add the scallions and shrimp to the wok and stir-fry for 2–3 minutes.

5 Stir in the soy sauce, lime juice, and noodles and mix well. Cook for 1 minute until thoroughly warmed through, then spoon into a warm serving dish, garnish with lime wedges, and serve immediately.

COOK'S TIP

Chinese egg noodles are made from
wheat or rice flour, water, and egg.
Noodles are a symbol of longevity,
and so are always served at birthday
celebrations—it is regarded as bad
luck to cut them.

VARIATION

This dish is just as tasty with
smaller cooked shrimp,
but it is not quite so
visually appealing.

Beef Chow Mein

Chow mein must be the best-known and most popular noodle dish on any Chinese menu. Beef is used in this recipe, but you could use chicken, pork, or vegetables instead.

Serves 4

INGREDIENTS

1 pound egg noodles	1 tsp grated fresh ginger root	8 scallions
4 tbsp peanut oil	1 green bell pepper, seeded and	1 tsp dark brown sugar
1 pound lean steak, cut into thin	thinly sliced	1 tbsp dry sherry
strips	1 carrot, peeled and thinly sliced	2 tbsp dark soy sauce
2 garlic cloves, crushed	2 celery stalks, sliced	few drops of chili sauce

1 Cook the noodles in a saucepan of boiling salted water for 4-5 minutes. Drain well, rinse under cold running water, and drain thoroughly again.

2 Toss the noodles in 1 tablespoon of the oil.

3 Heat the remaining oil in a preheated wok. Add the steak and stir-fry for 3-4 minutes, stirring constantly.

4 Add the garlic and ginger and stir-fry for 30 seconds.

5 Add the bell pepper, carrot, celery, and scallions and stir-fry for about 2 minutes.

6 Add the sugar, sherry, soy sauce, and chili sauce and cook, stirring occasionally, for 1 minute.

7 Stir in the noodles, mixing well, and cook for 1–2 minutes, or until completely warmed through.

8 Transfer to a warm serving bowl and serve immediately.

VARIATION

A variety of different vegetables may be used in this recipe for color and flavor—try broccoli, red bell peppers, green beans, or baby corncobs.

Cantonese Fried Noodles

This dish is usually served as a snack or light meal. It may also be served as an accompaniment to plain meat and fish dishes.

Serves 4

INGREDIENTS

12 ounces egg noodles
1¹/₂ pounds lean steak, cut into
   thin strips
3 tbsp vegetable oil

4¹/₂ ounces green cabbage, shredded
3 ounces bamboo shoots, drained
6 scallions, sliced
1 ounce green beans, halved
1 tbsp dark soy sauce

2 tbsp beef stock
1 tbsp dry sherry
1 tbsp light brown sugar
2 tbsp chopped fresh parsley,
   to garnish

1 Cook the noodles in a saucepan of boiling water for 2-3 minutes. Drain well, rinse under cold running water, and drain thoroughly again.

2 Heat 1 tablespoon of the oil in a preheated wok.

3 Add the noodles to the wok and stir-fry for 1-2 minutes. Drain and set aside until required.

4 Heat the remaining oil in the wok. Add the beef and stir-fry for 2-3 minutes.

5 Add the cabbage, bamboo shoots, scallions, and beans to the wok and stir-fry for about 1-2 minutes.

6 Add the soy sauce, stock, sherry, and sugar to the wok, stirring to mix well.

7 Stir the noodles into the mixture in the wok, tossing to mix well.

8 Transfer to serving bowls, garnish with chopped parsley, and serve immediately.

VARIATION

You can use lean pork or chicken instead of the beef in this recipe, if desired—remember to alter the stock accordingly.

Fried Noodles with Mushrooms & Pork

This dish benefits from the use of colored oyster mushrooms.
If these are unavailable, regular mushrooms will suffice.

Serves 4

INGREDIENTS

1 pound thin egg noodles
2 tbsp peanut oil
12 ounces pork tenderloin, sliced
2 garlic cloves, crushed
1 onion, cut into 8 sections

8 ounces oyster mushrooms
4 tomatoes, peeled, seeded, and
thinly sliced

2 tbsp light soy sauce
$1/4$ cup pork stock
1 tbsp chopped fresh cilantro

1 Cook the noodles in a saucepan of boiling water for 2-3 minutes. Drain well, rinse under cold running water, and drain thoroughly again.

2 Heat 1 tablespoon of the oil in a preheated wok.

3 Add the noodles to the wok and stir-fry for 2 minutes.

4 Using a slotted spoon, remove the noodles from the wok, drain well, and set aside until they are required.

5 Heat the remaining oil in the wok. Add the pork and stir-fry for 4-5 minutes.

6 Stir in the garlic and onion and stir-fry for a further 2-3 minutes.

7 Add the mushrooms, tomatoes, soy sauce, pork stock, and noodles. Stir well and cook for 1-2 minutes.

8 Transfer to a serving dish, sprinkle with chopped cilantro, and serve immediately.

COOK'S TIP

For crisper noodles, add 2 tablespoons of oil to the wok and fry the noodles for 5-6 minutes, turning them once halfway through cooking.

Lamb with Cellophane Noodles

Lamb is quick fried, coated in a soy sauce, and served on a bed of cellophane noodles for a richly flavored dish.

Serves 4

INGREDIENTS

5¹/₂ ounces cellophane noodles
2 tbsp peanut oil
1 pound lean lamb, thinly sliced

2 garlic cloves, crushed
2 leeks, sliced
3 tbsp dark soy sauce

1 cup lamb stock
dash of chili sauce
red chili strips, to garnish

1 Bring a large pan of water to a boil. Add the transparent noodles and cook for 1 minute. Drain the noodles well, rinse under cold running water, and drain thoroughly again.

2 Heat the peanut oil in a preheated wok. Add the lamb to the wok and stir-fry for about 2 minutes.

3 Add the garlic and leeks to the wok and stir-fry for a further 2 minutes.

4 Stir in the soy sauce, stock, and chili sauce and cook for 3-4 minutes, until the meat is cooked through.

5 Add the noodles to the wok and cook for 1 minute, until heated through.

6 Transfer to a serving dish, garnish, and serve.

COOK'S TIP

Chili sauce is a very hot sauce made from chilies, vinegar, sugar, and salt and should be used sparingly. Tabasco sauce can be used as a substitute.

COOK'S TIP

Cellophane noodles are available in Chinese grocery stores. Use egg noodles instead if cellophane noodles are unavailable, and cook them according to package instructions.

Cellophane Noodles with Shrimp

In this recipe, jumbo shrimp are cooked with orange juice, bell peppers, soy sauce, and vinegar and served on a bed of cellophane noodles for a truly wonderful dish.

Serves 4

INGREDIENTS

6 ounces cellophane noodles
1 tbsp vegetable oil
1 garlic clove, crushed
2 tsp grated fresh ginger root
24 raw jumbo shrimp, peeled and deveined

1 red bell pepper, seeded and thinly sliced
1 green bell pepper, seeded and thinly sliced
1 onion, chopped
2 tbsp light soy sauce
juice of 1 orange

2 tsp wine vinegar
pinch of brown sugar
$2/3$ cup fish stock
1 tbsp cornstarch
2 tsp water
orange slices, to garnish

1 Cook the noodles in a saucepan of boiling water for 1 minute. Drain well, rinse under cold water, and then drain thoroughly again.

2 Heat the oil in a preheated wok. Add the garlic and ginger and stir-fry for 30 seconds.

3 Add the shrimp and stir-fry for 2 minutes. Remove the

shrimp with a slotted spoon, set aside, and keep warm.

4 Add the bell peppers and onion to the wok and stir-fry for 2 minutes. Stir in the soy sauce, orange juice, vinegar, sugar, and stock.

5 Return the shrimp to the wok and cook for 8-10 minutes, until cooked through.

6 Blend the cornstarch with the water and add to the wok. Bring to a boil, add the noodles, and cook for 1-2 minutes. Garnish and serve immediately.

VARIATION

Lime or lemon juice and slices may be used instead of the orange. Use 3-5$1/2$ tsp of these juices.

Desserts

Desserts are almost unheard of in ordinary Chinese households and the following recipes are adaptations of Imperial recipes or use Chinese cooking methods and ingredients to produce delicious desserts that would round off any meal perfectly.

The Chinese do not usually have desserts to finish off a meal, except at banquets and special occasions. Sweet dishes are usually served in between main meals as snacks, but fresh fruit is considered to be very refreshing at the end of a big meal.

Rice is cooked with fruits, litchis are spiced with ginger and served with a refreshing orange sorbet, and wonton wrappers are sealed around a sweet date filling and laced with honey, to name but a few of the tempting treats that follow in this chapter.

Sweet Fruit Wontons

Sweet wontons are served mainly in restaurants and are not often found in a Chinese home. They are very adaptable and may be filled with whole, small fruits or a spicy chopped mixture, as here.

Serves 4

INGREDIENTS

12 wonton wrappers
2 tsp cornstarch
6 tsp cold water
oil, for deep-frying

2 tbsp clear honey
selection of fresh fruit (such as kiwi fruit, limes, oranges, mango, and apples), sliced, to serve

FILLING:
1 cup chopped dried, pitted dates
2 tsp dark brown sugar
$1/2$ tsp ground cinnamon

1 To make the filling, mix together the dates, sugar, and cinnamon in a bowl.

2 Spread out the wonton wrappers on a chopping board and spoon a little of the filling into the center of each wrapper.

3 Mix together the cornstarch and water and brush this around the edges of the wrappers.

4 Fold the wrappers over the filling, bringing the edges together, then bring the two corners together, sealing with the cornstarch mixture.

5 Heat the oil for deep-frying in a wok until a cube of bread browns in 30 seconds. Fry the wontons, in batches, for 2–3 minutes, until golden. Remove the wontons from the oil with a slotted spoon and drain thoroughly on absorbent paper towels.

6 Place the honey in a bowl and stand it in warm water, to soften it slightly. Meanwhile, arrange the wontons on a serving dish. Drizzle the honey over the wontons and serve immediately with the fresh fruit.

COOK'S TIP

Wonton wrappers may be found in Chinese grocery stores. Alternatively, make 1 quantity of the dough used for Shrimp Dumpling Soup (see page 24).

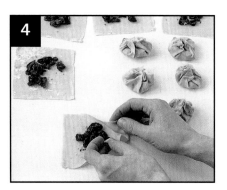

Banana Pastries

These pastries require a little time to prepare, but are well worth the effort.
A sweet banana filling is wrapped in dough and baked.

Serves 4

INGREDIENTS

DOUGH:
4 cups all-purpose flour
4 tbsp shortening
4 tbsp sweet butter
1/2 cup water

FILLING:
2 large bananas
1/3 cup finely chopped no-need-to-
    soak dried apricots
pinch of nutmeg

dash of orange juice
1 egg yolk, beaten
confectioners' sugar, for dusting
whipped cream or ice cream, to serve

1 To make the dough, sift the flour into a large mixing bowl. Add the shortening and butter and rub into the flour with your fingertips until the mixture resembles breadcrumbs. Gradually blend in the water to make a soft dough. Wrap in plastic wrap and chill in the refrigerator for 30 minutes.

2 Mash the bananas in a bowl with a fork and stir in the apricots, nutmeg, and orange juice, mixing well.

3 Roll the dough out on a lightly floured surface and cut out 4-inch rounds.

4 Spoon a little of the banana filling onto one half of each round and fold the dough over the filling to make semicircles. Pinch the edges together and seal by pressing with the prongs of a fork.

5 Arrange the pastries on a nonstick cookie sheet and brush them with the beaten egg yolk to glaze.

6 Cut a small slit in each pastry and cook in a preheated oven at 350°F for about 25 minutes, or until golden brown.

7 Dust with confectioners' sugar and serve with whipped cream or ice cream.

VARIATION

Use a fruit filling of your choice,
such as apple or plum, as an
alternative.

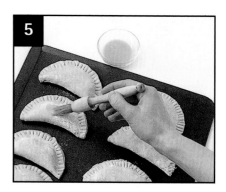

Mango Dumplings

*Fresh mango and canned litchis fill these small steamed dumplings,
making a really colorful and tasty treat.*

Serves 4

INGREDIENTS

DOUGH:
2 tsp baking powder
1 tbsp superfine sugar
$^2/_3$ cup water
$^2/_3$ cup milk

$3^1/_2$ cups all-purpose flour

FILLING:
1 small mango
4 ounce can litchis, drained

1 tbsp ground almonds
4 tbsp orange juice
ground cinnamon, for dusting

---

1 To make the dough, place the baking powder and sugar in a large mixing bowl. Mix the water and milk together and then stir this mixture into the baking powder and sugar mixture until well combined. Gradually stir in the flour to make a soft dough. Set the dough aside in a warm place for about 1 hour.

2 To make the filling, peel the mango and cut the flesh from the pit. Roughly chop the mango flesh; reserve half, and set aside for the sauce.

3 Chop the litchis and add to half of the chopped mango, together with the ground almonds. Let stand for 20 minutes.

4 Meanwhile, make the sauce. Blend the reserved mango and the orange juice in a food processor until smooth. Rub the mixture through a strainer to make a smooth sauce.

5 Divide the dough into 16 equal pieces. Roll each piece out on a lightly floured surface into 3-inch rounds.

6 Spoon a little of the mango and litchi filling onto the center of each round and fold the dough over the filling to make semicircles. Pinch the edges together to seal firmly.

7 Place the dumplings on a heatproof plate in a steamer, cover, and steam for about 25 minutes, until cooked through.

8 Remove the dumplings from the steamer, dust with a little ground cinnamon, and serve with the mango sauce.

Sweet Rice

*This dessert is served at banquets and celebratory meals
in China, as it looks wonderful when sliced.*

Serves 4

INGREDIENTS

3/4 cup round grain rice
2 tbsp sweet butter
1 tbsp superfine sugar
8 dried dates, pitted and chopped
1 tbsp raisins

5 candied cherries, halved
5 pieces angelica, chopped
5 walnut halves
1/2 cup canned chestnut purée

SYRUP:
2/3 cup water
2 tbsp orange juice
4 1/2 tsp light brown sugar
1 1/2 tsp cornstarch
1 tbsp cold water

1 Put the rice in a pan, cover with cold water, and bring to a boil. Reduce the heat, cover, and simmer for 15 minutes, or until the water has been absorbed. Stir in the butter and sugar.

2 Grease a 2½-cup heatproof bowl. Cover the base and sides with a thin layer of the rice, pressing it in firmly with the back of a spoon.

3 Mix the fruit and walnuts and press them into the rice.

4 Spread a thicker layer of rice on top and then fill the center with the chestnut purée. Cover with the remaining rice, pressing the top down to seal in the purée.

5 Cover the bowl with pleated wax paper and foil and secure with string tied around the rim. Place in a steamer, or stand the bowl in a pan and fill with hot water until it reaches halfway up the sides of the bowl. Cover and steam for 45 minutes. Let stand for 10 minutes.

6 Before serving, gently heat the water and orange juice. Add the sugar and stir to dissolve. Bring the syrup to a boil.

7 Mix the cornstarch with the cold water to form a smooth paste, then stir into the boiling syrup. Cook for 1 minute until thickened and clear.

8 Turn the pudding out onto a serving plate. Pour the syrup over the top, cut into slices, and serve immediately.

Honeyed Rice Puddings

These small rice puddings are quite sweet, but have a wonderful flavor because of the combination of ginger, honey, and cinnamon.

Serves 4

INGREDIENTS

1¹/₂ cups round grain rice
2 tbsp clear honey, plus extra
   for drizzling
large pinch of ground cinnamon

3 pieces preserved ginger,
   drained and chopped
15 no-need-to-soak dried
   apricots, chopped

8 whole no-need-to-soak dried
   apricots, to decorate

1 Put the rice in a saucepan and just cover with cold water. Bring to a boil, reduce the heat, cover, and cook for 15 minutes, or until the water has been absorbed.

2 Stir the honey and cinnamon into the rice.

3 Grease 4 × ²/₃-cup ramekin dishes or heatproof cups.

4 Blend the apricots and ginger in a food processor to make a paste. Divide the paste into 4 equal portions and shape each into a flat round to fit into the base of the cups.

5 Divide half the rice between the ramekins or cups and place the apricot paste on top.

6 Cover the apricot paste with the remaining rice. Cover the ramekins or cups with wax paper and foil and steam for 30 minutes, or until set.

7 Remove the ramekins or cups from the steamer and let stand for 5 minutes.

8 Turn the desserts out onto warm serving plates and drizzle with clear honey. Decorate with dried apricots and serve.

COOK'S TIP

The desserts may be left to chill in their ramekin dishes or cups in the refrigerator, then turned out and served with ice cream or whipped cream.

Mango Mousse

This is a light, softly set and tangy mousse, which is perfect for clearing the palate after a Chinese meal of mixed flavors.

Serves 4

INGREDIENTS

14 ounce can mangoes in syrup
2 pieces preserved ginger, drained
  and chopped
1 cup heavy cream

4 tsp powdered gelatin
2 tbsp water
2 egg whites
1½ tbsp light brown sugar

preserved ginger and lime zest,
  to decorate

1 Drain the mangoes, reserving the syrup. Blend the mango pieces and ginger in a food processor or blender for about 30 seconds, or until smooth.

2 Measure the purée and make up to 1¼ cups with the reserved mango syrup.

3 In a separate bowl, whip the cream until it forms soft peaks. Fold the mango mixture into the cream until combined.

4 Dissolve the gelatin in the water and let cool slightly.

Pour the gelatin into the mango mixture in a steady stream, stirring constantly. Let cool in the refrigerator for about 30 minutes, until almost set.

5 Beat the egg whites in a clean bowl until they form soft peaks, then beat in the sugar. Gently fold the egg whites into the mango mixture with a metal spoon.

6 Spoon the mousse into individual serving dishes or tall glasses and decorate with preserved ginger and lime zest. Serve immediately.

COOK'S TIP

The gelatin must be stirred into the mango mixture in a gentle, steady stream to prevent it from setting in lumps when it comes into contact with the cold mixture.

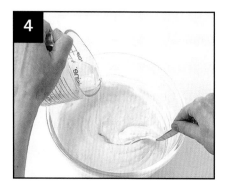

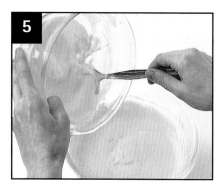

Poached Allspice Pears

These pears are moist and delicious after poaching in a sugar and allspice mixture.
They are wonderful served hot or cold.

Serves 4

INGREDIENTS

4 large, ripe pears
1¼ cups orange juice

2 tsp ground allspice
⅓ cup raisins

2 tbsp light brown sugar
grated orange rind, to decorate

1 Core and peel the pears and cut them in half.

2 Place the pear halves in a large saucepan.

3 Add the orange juice, allspice, raisins, and sugar to the pan and heat gently, stirring, until the sugar has dissolved. Bring the mixture to a boil for 1 minute.

4 Reduce the heat to low and simmer for about 10 minutes, or until the pears are cooked, but still fairly firm—test them by inserting the tip of a sharp knife.

5 Remove the pears from the pan with a slotted spoon and transfer to serving plates. Decorate and serve hot with the syrup.

COOK'S TIP

The Chinese do not usually have desserts to finish off a meal, except at banquets and special occasions. Sweet dishes are usually served in between main meals as snacks, but fruit is refreshing at the end of a big meal.

VARIATION

Use cinnamon instead of the allspice and decorate with cinnamon sticks and fresh mint sprigs, if desired.

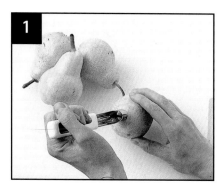

Chinese Custard Tarts

These small tarts are irresistible—a custard is baked in a rich, sweet pastry.
The tarts may be served warm or cold.

Makes 15

INGREDIENTS

DOUGH:
1¹/₂ cups all-purpose flour
3 tbsp superfine sugar
4 tbsp sweet butter
2 tbsp shortening
2 tbsp water

CUSTARD:
2 small eggs
¹/₄ cup superfine sugar
³/₄ cup milk

¹/₂ tsp ground nutmeg, plus extra
   for sprinkling
cream, to serve

1 To make the dough, sift the flour into a bowl. Add the sugar, butter, and shortening. Rub in the butter and shortening with your fingertips until the mixture resembles fine breadcrumbs. Add the water and mix to form a firm dough.

2 Transfer the dough to a lightly floured surface and knead for 5 minutes, until smooth. Cover with plastic wrap and chill in the refrigerator while you prepare the filling.

3 To make the custard, beat the eggs and sugar together. Gradually add the milk and ground nutmeg, beating constantly until well combined.

4 Separate the dough into 15 even-size pieces. Flatten the dough pieces into rounds and press into shallow tart pans.

5 Spoon the custard into the tart shells and cook in a preheated oven at 300°F for 25–30 minutes.

6 Transfer the tarts to a wire rack, let cool slightly, then sprinkle with nutmeg. Serve warm with cream.

COOK'S TIP

For extra convenience, make the dough in advance, cover, and chill in the refrigerator until required.

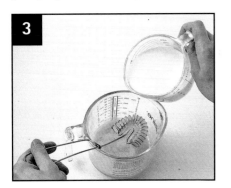

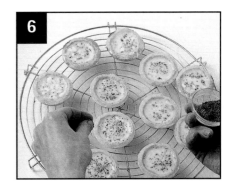

Ginger Litchis With Orange Sorbet

*This dish is truly delicious! The fresh flavor of the sorbet
perfectly complements the spicy litchis.*

Serves 4

INGREDIENTS

SORBET:

1¼ cups superfine sugar

2 cups cold water

12 ounce can mandarins, in
 natural juice

2 tbsp lemon juice

STUFFED LITCHIS:

15 ounce can litchis, drained

4 tbsp preserved ginger, drained and
 finely chopped

lime zest, cut into diamond shapes,
 to decorate

1 To make the sorbet, place the sugar and water in a saucepan and stir over a low heat until the sugar has dissolved. Bring the mixture to a boil and boil vigorously for 2–3 minutes.

2 Meanwhile, blend the mandarins in a food processor or blender until smooth. Rub the blended mandarin mixture through a strainer until smooth. Stir the mandarin sauce into the syrup, together with the lemon juice. Set aside to cool.

3 Pour the mixture into a rigid, plastic container suitable for the freezer and freeze until set, stirring occasionally.

4 Meanwhile, thoroughly drain the litchis on absorbent paper towels.

5 Spoon the chopped ginger into the center of the litchis.

6 Arrange the litchis on serving plates and serve with scoops of orange sorbet.

COOK'S TIP

It is best to leave the sorbet in the refrigerator for 10 minutes, so that it softens slightly, allowing you to scoop it to serve.

Deep-fried Bananas

*These bananas are quite irresistible, therefore it may be wise
to make double quantities!*

Serves 4

INGREDIENTS

8 medium bananas
2 tsp lemon juice
2/3 cup self-rising flour
2/3 cup rice flour

1 tbsp cornstarch
1/2 tsp ground cinnamon
1 cup water
4 tbsp light brown sugar

oil, for deep-frying

1 Cut the bananas into chunks and place them in a large mixing bowl.

2 Sprinkle the lemon juice over the bananas to prevent discoloration.

3 Sift the self-rising flour, rice flour, cornstarch, and cinnamon into a mixing bowl. Gradually stir in the water to make a thin batter.

4 Heat the oil in a preheated wok until almost smoking, then reduce the heat slightly.

5 Place a piece of banana on the end of a fork and carefully dip it into the batter, draining off any excess. Repeat with the remaining banana pieces.

6 Sprinkle the sugar onto a large plate.

7 Carefully place the banana pieces in the oil and cook for 2–3 minutes, until golden. Remove the banana pieces from the oil with a slotted spoon and roll them in the sugar. Transfer to serving bowls and serve with whipped cream or ice cream.

COOK'S TIP

Rice flour can be bought from whole-food stores or from Chinese grocery stores.

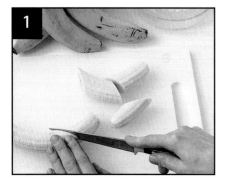

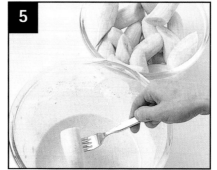

Index

Index compiled by Hilary Bird.